Mary, Queen of Scots:
Truth or Lies

For Anna Gordon, who loves history

Mary, Queen of Scots: Truth or Lies

ROSALIND K. MARSHALL

SAINT ANDREW PRESS
Edinburgh

First published in 2010 by
SAINT ANDREW PRESS
121 George Street
Edinburgh EH2 4YN

ISBN 978 0 7152 0936 3

British Library Cataloguing in Publication Data
A catalogue record for this book is available from the British Library

It is the Publisher's policy to only use papers that are natural and recyclable and that
have been manufactured from timber grown in renewable, properly managed forests.
All of the manufacturing processes of the papers are expected to conform to the
environmental regulations of the country of origin.

Typeset by Waverley Typesetters, Warham, Norfolk
Printed and bound by MPG Books, Bodmin

Contents

Events in the life of Mary, Queen of Scots

THE ENGLISH MONARCHY

Henry VIII reigned 1509–47
Edward VI reigned 1547–53
Mary I reigned 1553–8
Elizabeth I reigned 1558–1603

Chapter 1

Mary, Queen of Scots: A Frenchwoman or a Scot?

MYTH

Mary, Queen of Scots was the daughter of a Frenchwoman, Mary of Guise, who brought her up to speak nothing but French and then sent her to live in France when she was five years old. The two never saw each other again, and the little queen had no connection with Scotland after that, although she did have the Four Maries with her: Mary Seton, Mary Beaton, Mary Carmichael and Mary Hamilton. Eventually Mary, Queen of Scots married the Dauphin François, heir to the French throne, and by that time she had forgotten all about Scotland.

FACTS

Mary, Queen of Scots is often portrayed in films and plays dressed in French fashions and speaking English with a strong French accent. She was, after all, half-French, she had been brought up in France and her first husband was French. Apart from this slant lent to her life by romantic writers, some of her stern critics have chosen to give the impression that when she returned to rule Scotland in adult life she was to all intents and purposes a foreigner, totally ignorant of her native land and simply not interested in it. Was this a fair judgment? Did she have any sense of being Scottish at all and, if she did, how had that developed?

Mary became Queen of Scots in 1542 when she was six days old. Scotland was in crisis. Her father, James V, had died soon after his army had been defeated by the English at the Battle of Solway Moss, and now the country was left with an infant monarch amid fears of an invasion from the south. James Hamilton, Earl of Arran was appointed regent, with the title of Lord Governor; and at first he made peace with Henry VIII of England, promising that the baby queen would marry Henry's only son, Prince Edward, as soon as she was old enough. However, the Scots did not like the idea of an alliance with their old enemy, England, and so they broke the agreement. Henry VIII was furious at this change to his plans, and sent his army north to try to force the Scots to keep their promise. This was the first of the series of invasions known as the Rough Wooing, and during these years of conflict there were very real fears that the little queen would be kidnapped or even killed.

Mary's mother, Mary of Guise, came from Lorraine, on the eastern border of France, and she had arrived in Scotland in 1538 as a young widow to marry James V. A tall and commanding figure with a personality to match, she had been a reluctant bride, not least because she had to leave behind with her parents her young son by her first husband. However, she had quickly adapted to life in her new country and she learned to speak fluent Scots, although John Knox mocked her for having a strong French accent. She and James V had two sons, both of whom died in infancy, and so it was not surprising that she was fiercely protective of her last child, whom she named after herself.

Instead of speaking to her daughter in her own native language, it seems that Mary of Guise made sure that the little girl spoke only Scots. After all, the child would presumably rule Scotland for herself one day. The priority during these years was to make sure that she survived. The threat to her safety increased when the English defeated the Scots at the Battle of Pinkie in 1547, and so when Henri II of France suggested a marriage between Mary, Queen of Scots and his own son and heir, the Dauphin François, Mary of Guise was eager to agree. From Henri's point of view, this would strengthen still further his country's traditional alliance with Scotland.

Admittedly, Scotland was a much smaller, poorer nation but, when France was at war with England, it was always useful to have the Scots create a diversion by marching an army across the Border. Henri wanted the little queen to be brought up with his own children at his court. This would mean a very painful parting for Mary of Guise, but her main concern was that her daughter should be safe and would have a glittering future as queen consort of France. Of course there were those Scots who opposed the idea, but the Regent Arran was soon persuaded to agree when Henri offered him a French dukedom. He accepted with alacrity, becoming Duke of Châtelherault, the only duke in Scotland.

On 7 August 1548, at the age of five, Mary, Queen of Scots therefore set sail for France. She was escorted by a number of the Scottish nobility who would return as soon as they had seen her safely installed, and by various other Scots who would stay on with her to form part of her own royal household. Henri II was determined to transform his future daughter-in-law into a Frenchwoman, but her mother remained clear about her status. She was Queen of Scots in her own right and she must have Scots about her to emphasise her position as well as to make her feel more comfortable in a strange land. Henri liked and respected Mary of Guise and so he agreed that, although her daughter would live with his children, she would be served for the most part by her own attendants. Some were Scots and others were French. Mary of Guise paid 50,000 livres a year for their upkeep, while Henri added a further 30,000 livres.

We know from household lists of the time that, during her first ten years in France, Mary usually had fifteen male indoor servants and from twelve to fourteen female attendants. The men, who saw her less often, included her French dancing master and Claude Millot, her schoolmaster. The women were her close companions and ten of the fourteen were Scots. There was her nurse, Jean Sinclair, and there were ladies-in-waiting, maids of honour and chamberwomen. In charge of them was Mary's aunt, Jane Stewart, Lady Fleming. Jane was the illegitimate daughter of Mary's grandfather, King James IV. She had been married off to Malcolm, 3rd Lord Fleming, when she was in her mid-teens and he was over 30. They had two sons and six daughters, and Lady Fleming was a lively and familiar figure at the Scottish court.

Less than a year before Mary's voyage to France, Lord Fleming had been killed at the Battle of Pinkie. His eight children were growing up now, and his vivacious widow would probably welcome a change of scene. Mary of Guise therefore chose Lady Fleming to be the little queen's governess. This word had a different meaning in the sixteenth century. The governess of a royal child did not give her lessons but would be the closest person to her and, since Lady Fleming was also Mary's aunt, she would have enough influence to intervene if the French were not treating her niece with proper respect. Her two youngest daughters went with her. One of them, named Mary, was about the same age as Mary, Queen of Scots and she became one of the famous Four Maries, four little girls all called Mary, who would be in attendance on the queen.

The fact that all four were called Mary is not really such a surprising coincidence. Scotland was a Roman Catholic country when they were born, and many girls were called after the Virgin Mary, mother of Jesus Christ. What is more, documents show that previous Scottish queens also had female attendants who were known as their Maries, regardless of what their first names were. John Jamieson, a nineteenth-century Scottish minister who compiled a large and comprehensive dictionary of the Scots language, believed that the term came from an Icelandic word, *mær*, which meant a virgin or maid and this seems to be a convincing explanation.

Whatever the origin of the word, the four girls were to be maids of honour to Mary, Queen of Scots. When they were older, they would be promoted to be ladies-in-waiting. Over the years there has been a good deal of confusion about the identity of this very special quartet. They were in fact Mary Fleming, Mary Beaton, Mary Seton and Mary Livingston. There was no Mary Hamilton, and there was no Mary Carmichael. These two names come from an old, fictitious Scottish ballad published by Sir Walter Scott. It tells the sad tale of a young woman executed for murdering her illegitimate baby, and it became very popular, but it had nothing to do with the real Four Maries.

Maids of honour were usually chosen from aristocratic families who were particularly loyal to the crown, and in this instance there also seem to have been personal connections involved. Like Mary Fleming, the most important of the Maries, they were all about the same age as the queen herself. Mary Seton would no doubt have been selected because her mother, Marie Pierres, was one of the French ladies-in-waiting who had accompanied Mary of Guise to Scotland ten years earlier. Less than a year after her arrival, she had married George, 4th Lord Seton, a widower with a grown-up family and with him she had two sons and this small daughter. Mary Beaton had a similar background. Her father, Robert Beaton of Creich, was not a member of the nobility, but his wife, Jeanne de la Rainville, was another of Mary of Guise's French ladies-in-waiting. The final Marie was Mary Livingston, daughter of Alexander, 5th Lord Livingston, one of the official guardians of Mary, Queen of Scots.

The small girls were companions of the queen on her stormy voyage to France, and it is sometimes said that when they arrived they were cruelly separated from her by the French king. According to comments made when Henri II first saw Mary, Queen of Scots, it seems that he was concerned because she did not speak French, and he gave orders that her Maries were to be sent away. If she was always surrounded by Scots, she would never become a fluent speaker of French herself, he allegedly remarked. He may well have said this, but the measures he took were not nearly as drastic as they sound. While Mary, Queen of Scots received from her tutors the fine education suitable for a Renaissance monarch, the girls were to go to the imposing Priory of St Louis at Poissy, where they would be taught under the supervision of the Dominican prioress, Françoise de Vieuxpoint.

Poissy was only a few kilometres from St Germain, where the French royal children usually stayed and so the girls were not being exiled to some remote place. Instead, it was an important opportunity for them, for the Priory had a fine reputation. In the fourteenth century, an aunt of King Charles VI of France had been its prioress and Christine de Pizan, the celebrated early fifteenth-century writer, sent her daughter Marie to the Priory and then spent the last eleven years of her own life there. Apparently the absence of the Maries had the desired effect, for Mary, Queen of Scots soon became a fluent speaker of French. She composed all her personal letters in that language, and they are far more fluent and expansive than the ones she wrote in Scots. Indeed, it is evident from her correspondence that she came to think in French, as befitted a future queen of France.

Even so, her Guise uncles and her other relatives constantly stressed the fact that she was a monarch in her own right, and in so doing they naturally emphasised her Scottish identity. Also, Mary was kept in constant touch with her own country by means of the steady stream of messengers passing between the two courts in France and Scotland. This regular contact mattered a great deal to her, because she was always anxious to have news of Mary of Guise. The Venetian ambassador once remarked that she loved her mother 'incredibly', much more than daughters usually did. The two were determined to see each other again as soon as possible. It was, of course, difficult for Mary of Guise to leave Scotland because of the unstable situation there, but in 1550 she managed it. One of her principal reasons for making the long journey was that she was determined to replace the Earl of Arran as regent, and she needed the support of Henri II if she was to succeed. However, her daughter was probably at the forefront of her mind and, as soon as she landed at Dieppe on 19 September, her brothers took her to Rouen, where Mary was waiting. The reunion must have delighted both of them.

Mary of Guise stayed as an honoured guest at the French court throughout that winter. She was involved in complicated political discussions, of course, but she saw as much of the little queen as she possibly could. She would have to return to Scotland in the spring, when the galleys could take to the water again, but just as she was making her preparations for the voyage, some horrifying news was brought to her. A plan to poison Mary, Queen of Scots had been uncovered. Mary of Guise fell ill with shock, and not only did she postpone her departure but she stayed on for a further six months so that, in all, mother and daughter were together for just over a year. She finally set out in October 1551, no doubt with promises to young Mary that she would return as soon as she could. The year they had spent together must have deepened their already close relationship.

After that, Mary, Queen of Scots soon grew old enough to write letters to her mother. At first these were short and formal, more like schoolroom exercises than anything else, but as the months went by they became more personal in tone. After Mary of Guise finally wrested the regency from the Earl of Arran in 1554, she was visibly instructing her daughter on how to rule Scotland. She described her own current problems, making the young queen familiar with the names and personalities of the Scottish courtiers, asked her formally for approval of what she had done, and encouraged her to make suggestions of her own. Why did she bother? Twice widowed and having lost four of her five children, Mary of Guise knew all about the uncertainties of life and she worried constantly that her daughter's marriage might never take place. Royal betrothals had fallen through in the past, if the two monarchs involved quarrelled with each other or found a better partner for their son or daughter. This must not be allowed to happen; but, if it did, Mary, Queen of Scots would have to return to her native land and rule the country for herself.

As the years went by, her mother's situation grew more and more dangerous in the face of the increasingly hostile Protestants and the general opposition to all the improvements that the queen regent was trying to make. Her authority was constantly being challenged. With a great sense of relief, Mary of Guise learned that Henri II had finally announced that the wedding of his son and her daughter would take place in April 1558. She was determined to attend this momentous occasion in person and she publicly announced her plans. It was a bitter disappointment when a new series of crises erupted and she dared not leave Scotland. The magnificent wedding at Notre Dame Cathedral in Paris took place on 24 April 1558 without her.

Mary, Queen of Scots loved her new husband, perhaps more as a friend than as a romantic partner. François had always been delicate and undersized, and she seems to have felt protective of him. Just over a year after their marriage, she became queen of France when her father-in-law Henri II was fatally wounded in a jousting accident and her husband succeeded him as François II. She needed no coronation, for she was already a crowned and anointed queen. François had by this time matured and grown much more manly in appearance, while Mary made the ideal consort: tall, charming and glamorous. Her future seemed assured. She would remain by his side, overseeing the upbringing of their children when they came along, while her mother would continue to rule Scotland for her.

The following year everything changed. To Mary's great grief, her mother died on 11 June 1560, worn out by her efforts to modernise Scotland and keep it within the Roman Catholic Church. Less than six months after that, François II died of an abscess on the brain following an ear infection. A foreign bride had the choice of staying in her new country or returning home. Mary of Guise had chosen to remain where she was, but Mary, Queen of Scots was a queen in her own right, and that was rather different. There was now a strong expectation that she would go back to her native land and begin to rule it for herself. Her uncles did not want her to do that, because it was through her that they had built up significant power and influence at the French court.

However, she made up her own mind, and she decided to return to the country of her birth.

The prospect must have been unappealing in many ways, but Mary had never been allowed to forget her own background, and she had no problem with the notion of a dual nationality. From her first week of life, she had been queen of Scots and now, at 18, she was also queen dowager of France. Her strong sense of identity would remain unchanged throughout the dramas of her adult life and, twenty-six years on, escorted to the scaffold at Fotheringhay, she would tell her steward to let her friends know that she died a true Scotswoman and a true Frenchwoman.

Chapter 2

Mary, Queen of England?

MYTHS

Mary, Queen of Scots went back to Scotland after her first husband died because she was determined to get the English throne for herself, even though she had no claim to it at all. She was simply wanting to make trouble for Queen Elizabeth I of England.

FACTS

We are accustomed to the name 'Mary, Queen of Scots', but should she also have been Mary, Queen of England? This may sound a far-fetched notion, but there is no doubt that many people in the sixteenth century believed that she was the rightful English queen. Indeed, she had been brought up to think so herself and the possibility was to haunt the rest of her life. Was it all a delusion, or did she have a realistic claim? To understand the situation, we have to set aside thoughts of Mary Stuart for the moment and look back at the history of the English royal family.

In 1485 Henry Tudor ended England's Wars of the Roses by defeating King Richard III at the Battle of Bosworth and taking the crown for himself. As King Henry VII, he became the first Tudor monarch and to strengthen his position he quickly married one of his rivals for the throne, Princess Elizabeth of York. A year later their first son, Prince Arthur, was born, and they went on to have three other children who survived to adult life: Henry, Margaret and Mary. Arthur, a premature baby, grew into a delicate child but, when he was less than a year old, his father had already begun to plan his marriage. Henry VII was anxious to secure his hold on the crown still further by making a series of foreign alliances and so, when King Ferdinand of Aragon offered his baby daughter Catherine as a bride for Arthur, Henry was enthusiastic. Complicated negotiations dragged on for years, but the young couple were finally married by proxy when Arthur was 13 and Catherine a year older. Small, plump and devout, she arrived in England two years after that. Following a wedding ceremony in St Paul's Cathedral, this time with the bride and groom present, she and her husband were sent to live in Ludlow Castle, on the Welsh border. Four months later, Arthur died of tuberculosis.

What was to become of Catherine? Should she be sent back to Spain, or should she stay in England? The answer seemed obvious to Henry VII, who did not want to lose the dowry she had brought with her. She should marry his younger son instead. Prince Henry was a fine, sturdy boy, Catherine's father was agreeable, and so on 23 June 1503 a treaty for their marriage was signed. Catherine was 17, her bridegroom was 12, and they were supposed to marry as soon as he reached the age of 15. However, it took much longer than that. Henry VII kept thinking of other, more suitable wives for his heir, and it was only after his death in 1509 that the wedding finally took place.

At first, husband and wife were delighted with each other. Henry was tall, athletic and intelligent, and Catherine was gratifyingly devoted to him. However, as the years went by, she failed in what was seen as her principal duty, to provide him with an heir. She suffered miscarriages and stillbirths, her baby boys died in infancy and her only living child was a girl, Princess Mary Tudor. Henry had long since tired of his ailing, ageing wife and he was desperate for a son. When he fell in love with the dark-haired and alluring Anne Boleyn, he decided that he would put away his wife and marry Anne instead. He therefore asked the pope to declare his marriage to Catherine null and void. Catherine had been his brother's wife, and a relationship with her was forbidden by the Bible. The pope refused; and, although Catherine had powerful relatives – her nephew was Charles V, the Holy Roman Emperor – Henry decided to go ahead anyway. Possibly encouraged by Protestant Anne, he broke with Rome, made himself head of the Church of England, and secretly married her when she told him that she was pregnant. The baby, born on 7 September 1533, was a daughter. Henry named her Elizabeth, after his mother.

These events divided not only England but also Western Europe. Catholics angrily pointed out that Henry had no right to put aside his lawful wife. His wedding to Anne meant nothing. She was only his mistress, and her child was illegitimate. Henry's matrimonial adventures did not end there, however. In 1536 Catherine of Aragon died of cancer and he rejoiced. The danger of her nephew, the emperor, invading England on her behalf had gone. Henry appeared the next day dressed from head to foot in celebratory yellow but, at the very time of Catherine's funeral, Anne had a miscarriage. When her women reported that the child would have been a boy, Henry was furious with her for what he saw as her carelessness, and he became morbidly obsessed with the thought that God was punishing him for having married his brother's widow. He resolved to find another wife.

The Bishop of London was shocked when Henry raised the subject of a divorce, and so the king found an alternative way of freeing himself from Anne. He had her arrested and executed on charges of adultery and treason, and then he married quiet, undemanding Jane Seymour instead. On 12 October 1537 Jane gave birth to a son, Edward, and Henry had his male heir at last. However, Jane died of puerperal fever less than a fortnight later. Henry would marry three more times but he had no more children, and his erratic married life had made the succession to the English throne a matter of uncertainty and bitter dispute.

When Henry died in 1547, his three children were still alive: Mary, Elizabeth and Edward. A few days earlier, Henry had dictated a will leaving the throne to his son, who now became Edward VI. On the face of it, that seemed reasonable enough, because a son would always inherit, even if he had older sisters. If Edward died childless, the throne would then go to Mary, and if she too had no children, it would pass to Elizabeth. What would happen if Elizabeth also died childless? There were not many members of the Tudor royal family left, for Henry's sisters had died before him. However, they had both left descendants, and so, in the unlikely event of none of his own children having heirs, Henry wanted the family of his younger sister, Mary, Duchess of Suffolk to come next in the succession. In so doing, he was passing over the descendants of his older sister, Margaret, presumably because she had married a foreigner, King James IV of Scotland.

Needless to say, Henry's will was highly controversial because of the religious complications. Catholics wanted his daughter Princess Mary to succeed him, since in their view she was his only legitimate child. It was illegal for an illegitimate son or daughter to inherit anything. Protestants, of course, supported Edward, a promising youth, devoted to the Reformed faith. The Scots and the French argued that Henry's will was totally invalid because he had been too ill to sign it. Instead, a copy of his signature had been stamped on it, a procedure not unknown for state documents but inappropriate to a will.

Despite all these arguments, Prince Edward succeeded his father as King Edward VI. However, he died only six years later, in the summer of 1553, probably of tuberculosis and, in keeping with the terms of their father's will, his half-sister Princess Mary succeeded him. Brought up by her devout Catholic mother, she subsequently married Philip II of Spain and began persecuting the English Protestants. Her health was poor, however, and already thoughts were turning to her successor. Again according to Henry VIII's will, her half-sister Princess Elizabeth should succeed her, but, for Catholics everywhere, Elizabeth remained no more than the illegitimate daughter of Anne Boleyn, Henry's mistress. She had no right to rule over England. So, who was the real heir?

Henri II of France thought that he knew the answer. The true queen of England was his own daughter-in-law, Mary, Queen of Scots. He knew all about Henry VIII's will, and he was well aware that Henry had had two sisters. For him, however, Margaret, the elder, was the important one, simply because she had been born first. Henry might have meant to pass over her descendants, but dynastic rules were dynastic rules, and even the arrogant king of England could not alter that. Margaret's marriage to James IV, King of Scots in 1503 had been arranged in an attempt to make peace between their two countries. 'The marriage of the Thistle and the Rose', people called it. James was more than twice Margaret's age, but as well as being an energetic and imaginative intellectual, he was affable and he liked women. He was kind to his little bride, and, although only one of their children survived infancy, he made no attempt to replace his wife.

Fortunately, that baby was a son, and when James IV was killed fighting against the English at the Battle of Flodden in 1513, the child succeeded to the throne of Scotland as James V. Throughout his reign, he was on consistently bad terms with his uncle, Henry VIII of England. He died in 1542, leaving a daughter, Mary, Queen of Scots. She had inherited not only her father's kingdom but also his place in the English succession and now, because of the dwindling away of the royal family in England, Henri took the view that Mary was the senior claimant to the English throne. As far as he was concerned, a trifling consideration like Henry VIII's will was not going to spoil his plans.

Henri was not, of course, acting out of kindness to his son's young fiancée. England and France had long been enemies, but Scotland was France's traditional ally, and a useful one at that. The danger was that, with the spread of Protestantism in Scotland, the Scots might decide to break their Auld Alliance with the French and seek the friendship of Protestant England instead. In fact, that was exactly what was happening now, and that was why it had been vital for Mary of Guise to stay on in Scotland as regent for her daughter, fighting off any attempts by the English to infiltrate Scotland. By 1558, when Mary I of England's reign was drawing to a close, Mary of Guise's position was becoming increasingly difficult and she was in poor health. Henri II was aware of this, but he reasoned that, if Mary, Queen of Scots could succeed Mary Tudor on the throne of England, then the threat to French security from the other side of the Channel would be permanently removed. After his own death, France, Scotland and England would be united, with Mary, Queen of Scots and her husband François ruling all three.

In the spring of that same year, 1558, Henri II furthered his plans when the marriage contract between Mary, Queen of Scots and his son François was drawn up. François was to have the title of King of Scots. Henri wanted the Scottish crown to be sent to France so that his son could be crowned as such. Worried at the prospect of their country being taken over by the French, the Scots declined, but they did agree the following year that François should be granted the crown matrimonial, which meant that he was not simply a king consort but would rule Scotland jointly with his wife. After that, the signatures of both king and queen were needed for all Scottish state documents, and it was noticeable that François always signed on the left, the more important position. Of course, this was the accepted place for a husband's signature but, in the case of a queen in her own right, that would not usually have been the way to do it.

Even more significantly, on 4 April 1558, 15-year-old Mary, Queen of Scots signed a secret treaty with the French before she put her name to her marriage contract. In its three documents, she agreed that, if she were to die without children, she would bequeath to France both Scotland and her rights to the English throne. At the same time, she put her kingdom in pledge to Henri until the Scots paid him back the very large sums of money he had spent in defending them against the English. In the third deed, she annulled in advance any promises the Scots might force her to make which were contrary to these agreements. Mary did not sign the secret treaty on her own initiative, of course. Her uncles, the Duke of Guise and the Cardinal of Lorraine, were involved in the negotiation of the terms and her mother would have known all about them too. She and the rest of the Guise family presumably rejoiced that an even more glorious future awaited Mary, Queen of Scots as monarch of three kingdoms.

Mary's critics have seen the signing of the secret treaty as an act of treachery on her part, while her defenders have tried to excuse her by arguing that she was too young to realise the implications and was merely doing what her family told her to do. Seven months after her marriage, on 17 November 1558, Mary I of England died, and Henri II immediately saw his opportunity. He had Mary, Queen of Scots publicly proclaimed in Paris as queen of England, Scotland and

Ireland, and she and her husband added the English coat of arms to their own. At a lavish display of jousting at the end of June 1559, two heralds wore purple velvet displaying the new coat of arms. Henri II was fatally wounded in this tournament, and he died on 10 July. The day after that, the English ambassador heard that Mary had written to Scotland to say that she was now queen of France and Scotland, and hoped to be queen of England too.

Less than a year later, Mary of Guise died, worn out by her long years of struggle. By this time, Scotland had become a battleground for the French soldiers sent to help her and the English soldiers dispatched by Elizabeth I to support the Scottish Protestants. The following month, on 6 July 1560, France and England signed the Treaty of Edinburgh. By its terms all foreign troops were to leave Scotland and Mary, Queen of Scots and her husband would recognise Elizabeth I as the rightful queen of England by ceasing to quarter the English arms with their own. François II died five months after that, on 5 December 1560.

So what would Mary do now? At first, her thoughts did not turn to Scotland. She was deeply upset by the death of her husband, but a queen in her own right was a valuable prize on the marriage market, and her uncles were eager for her to take a new husband as soon as possible. They were determined that the bridegroom should be a king or the son of a king, and Mary shared their views on the subject. As the daughter and the wife of kings, she felt that she could accept no one of lower status as a second husband. They fixed on the idea of King Philip II of Spain's son, Don Carlos, as the best possible candidate. Unfortunately for their plans, Philip proved impossible to convince. He already had an alliance with France, sealed by his recent marriage to Henri II's daughter Elisabeth, and, in any event, Don Carlos's poor health made him unlikely to be a suitable husband for anyone. The question of Mary returning to Scotland then began to play an important part in thoughts about her future.

Some historians have argued that Mary wanted to stay on in France in the hope of marrying the Spanish heir, while others have suggested that she was eager to leave because she did not like being overshadowed by her domineering mother-in-law. Catherine de Medici was now ruling France as regent for her next son, Charles IX, and this meant that Mary would have to take second place to her. More importantly, Catherine was opposed to the idea of a Spanish marriage, reputedly fearing that her own daughter, Elisabeth, would somehow be pushed aside by the more glamorous Mary. Catherine was a notorious plotter, and Mary knew that she would have more freedom of action if she left France. There were, however, enormous problems to that. Apart from the fact that her ambitious Guise relatives did not want to see her disappearing to a small country on the northern edge of the world, her friends were quick to point out that, by a series of acts in August 1560, the Scottish parliament had made that country officially Protestant. How could a Catholic Queen possibly rule a Protestant land unless she returned at the head of an army to drive out her enemies?

In the spring of 1561, two Scottish envoys came to see Mary while she was visiting her Guise relatives in the north-east of France. The Scottish Catholics sent John Leslie, future

Bishop of Ross, to urge her to come to the north of Scotland and overthrow the Protestants, restoring Catholicism once more. They assured her that the powerful Catholic Earl of Huntly and his friends in the north-east would support her. Mary refused. Her other Scottish visitor was her Protestant half-brother, one of her father's many illegitimate sons. Lord James Stewart, later Earl of Moray, was an impressive figure, an experienced man of 30 who was royal in all but name. But for the accident of birth, he, instead of Mary, would have inherited the Scottish throne. He was a convinced Protestant, and he had come to see what she intended doing. His friends might be alarmed at the prospect of her return, which they believed would be a disaster, but he intended to invite her to come back to her kingdom, probably seeing himself as ruling on behalf of a very young and ingenuous half-sister.

Lord James spent five days with Mary, and, although we have no formal account of their conversations, it seems that she agreed that she would go back to Scotland and recognise the Reformed Church on the understanding that she could attend Catholic services in private. Jenny Wormald the historian, who is highly critical of Mary, thinks that Lord James must have persuaded her to go back by promising that he would support her claim to the English throne. This is speculation, of course, but it is a plausible theory. Mary would always say that she had no intention of trying to depose Elizabeth. She simply wanted to be nominated as her heir and that certainly would have seemed a much more achievable aim if she could negotiate as queen in her own right from her own country. We will probably never know what part the English claim really played in her thinking. It does seem that while she was in France she was very much following the policy laid down by Henri II; but, as we shall see in Chapter 8, once she was in Scotland her negotiations with Elizabeth took on a much more personal tone. Whatever her thoughts on the subject of the English succession, it is generally accepted that the decision to go back was entirely her own.

When Lord James left, Mary went to Paris to make preparations for her departure. Knowing that her voyage home would take her along the east coast of England, she sent to ask Elizabeth I for a safe conduct in case she should be driven ashore by bad weather. When the request was put before her, Elizabeth flew into a rage and demanded to know if Mary had ratified the Treaty of Edinburgh, recognising Elizabeth as queen. She had not, and so no safe conduct was forthcoming. When the English ambassador in France visited Mary soon afterwards, she told him that her preparations were so far advanced that she could not think of cancelling her journey. If she was captured at sea and taken to Elizabeth, the English queen would be able to do what she liked with her. Always fond of a dramatic turn of phrase, she added that, if she desired Mary's end, then Elizabeth could do as she wished and sacrifice her. With that, Mary set sail for Scotland on 14 August 1561.

Chapter 3

What did Mary and John Knox really think of each other?

MYTH

When Mary, Queen of Scots met John Knox, they immediately fell out because he was a crusty old man who hated all women. He bullied her and she, young and eager to please, burst into tears whenever she saw him. Because she was so beautiful, it could even be that he was secretly attracted to her and trying to conceal it.

FACTS

Most people know that Mary, Queen of Scots and John Knox were bitter enemies. Her supporters like to think of him as a fierce, bad-tempered bully who shouted at her, preached against her and nastily reduced her to tears. A famous nineteenth-century picture shows her sitting uncomfortably in a pew listening to him as he roars out his complaints about her behaviour. Her critics, on the other hand, believe that she was an empty-headed young woman who had no idea of who he was or what he was trying to do and, through sheer stupidity, almost sabotaged his work. So where does the reality lie? Did the queen and the leading preacher of the newly Reformed Church of Scotland really hate each other and, if so, whose fault was it?

The accounts of what passed between them come from Knox's own descriptions in his history of the Reformation in Scotland. In that book he made no secret of his feelings when he heard of Mary's return. There was a thick fog when she sailed into Leith on 19 August 1561, the sort of east-coast haar which is all too familiar in that part of the country even today. Knox thought it a bad omen. The very sky showed what sorrow and darkness the queen was bringing with her, he said. The sun did not shine for two days before or two days after her arrival, because God was warning people about what was going to happen. Mary would try to restore Roman Catholicism in Scotland, and to him that was an unbearable prospect. He would do everything he could to stop her.

When he heard that she was going to attend mass in the Chapel Royal in the Palace of Holyroodhouse on her very first Sunday in Scotland, Knox must have felt that his worst fears were justified. Of course, what she was doing was perfectly in keeping with the arrangements made when she agreed to return to her native land. She would not interfere with the Reformed Church but she would be allowed to worship as she chose. The following Sunday, Knox made his own views plain when he preached against Roman Catholicism, declaring that one mass was more alarming to him than an invasion by 10,000 foreign soldiers sent to suppress the true religion.

Two days later, Mary made her formal entry into Edinburgh. The first time a monarch entered the capital was always a great occasion, with a long royal procession, people in fancy dress, fountains flowing with wine and, every so often along the route, entertaining pageants. At one point, a painted cloud was lowered as if from the sky and a small child emerged from it to hand the queen not only the keys to Edinburgh, as tradition demanded, but also two books bound in rich purple velvet. When she opened them, she discovered that one was a copy of the Bible in English and the other was a psalm book. Both these books were unmistakable symbols of the Reformed religion. The Bibles that Mary knew were in Latin, but Protestants were insisting that the Word of God should be in a language that everyone could understand. Likewise, the singing of psalms had replaced the elaborate choral music of Catholic Church services.

Mary had no hesitation in believing that John Knox was responsible for these inappropriate gifts. She might have been in Edinburgh for only a very short time, but she knew all about him. As we have seen, during her French years she had been kept closely informed of what was happening in Scotland. In the late 1550s, when her mother's position as regent was threatened and Knox was preaching his spirited sermons against Catholicism, Mary followed events closely and with much anxiety, desperately worried about Mary of Guise's health and the threat to her from the combined Protestant armies of Scotland and England.

Now, determined to see Knox for herself and rebuke him for the impertinence of this latest gesture, Mary summoned him to Holyroodhouse. Their first encounter took place on 4 September 1561, a fortnight after her return. Physical appearance is an important element in first impressions, and the queen and the preacher could hardly have been more different. Like her mother and her French uncles, Mary was unusually tall, about six feet in height. She must have towered over Knox, who was of medium size, probably around five feet five, since most sixteenth-century people were smaller than we are today. She was 18, he was about 50. She still wore mourning for her dead husband, but her garments would have been made of expensive fabrics and she would almost certainly have been wearing her usual gold crucifix with, perhaps, a rosary. Like other ministers of the Reformed Church at that period, Knox would have been soberly dressed in dark, everyday clothes: a doublet and hose and, if it was chilly, a gown, which was the equivalent of a modern coat. A verbal description of the time records that he had dark hair, a ruddy complexion, a fairly short dark beard flecked with grey, and piercing dark blue eyes.

From her authentic portraits (there are many others which are imaginary, or of a much later date), we can see that Mary's hair was dark auburn, her eyes brown and her nose fairly large and aquiline. French poets had enthusiastically praised her beauty and seemed particularly taken with her flawless complexion. Her charm of manner impressed almost everyone who met her but, to Knox, her youthful beauty concealed a devious nature. Some historians have come up with the theory that he was hostile to her because he was secretly attracted to her, but this is to misread his motives. He had no personal interest in her physical appearance or her personality. For him, she was the dangerous enemy of the Reformed Church.

For her part, Mary considered, as her mother had done, that his religion was no more than a cloak for political machinations, and she thought that all his talk about the Word of God and the faults of the Catholic Church was simply an excuse for his desire to overthrow the monarchy. Mary believed that she ruled over Scotland because God had given her this sacred task, while Knox was convinced that God had called him to rescue the Scots from sin and bring them back to obedience. Mary realised, of course, that she could not simply order him to be thrown into prison for his impertinence, because that would have wrecked her policy of religious toleration.

Knox was an establishment figure, the respected minister of St Giles', Edinburgh's parish church, occupying his comfortable manse nearby and enjoying a salary of £200 a year, the highest amount payable to a minister. Although he has recently been portrayed as 'a man of the people', he seems to have come from a family of well-to-do merchants or craftsmen in Haddington, East Lothian and, although he was orphaned at an early age, the relatives who took him in were able to afford to have him educated locally and then sent to St Andrews University so that he could take his degree and become a priest, the usual career path for an intelligent boy at that time.

There were too many priests in Scotland already for the size of the population and so when he graduated he did not find a parish but became an apostolic notary – in other words, a country lawyer – back in the Haddington area. His own writings do not describe his conversion to the Reformed faith, but we know that in the early 1540s he became a follower of George Wishart, the famous Protestant preacher. When Wishart was burned at the stake for heresy in 1546 Knox had to go into hiding, in fear of his own life. After some months he joined a group of Protestants who had taken refuge in St Andrews Castle, but they were captured and carried off to France, where Knox was forced to become a galley slave. When he was finally released, he did not dare go back to Scotland because he would have been in danger of suffering the same fate as Wishart and so he went to Protestant England instead.

There he became a famous and popular pastor, and was even offered the bishopric of Rochester. He refused this because, as he explained afterwards, he could foresee trouble ahead, and he was right. When fervently Roman Catholic Mary Tudor inherited the English throne and began persecuting Protestants, Knox fled to the continent and made his way to Geneva. Becoming the friend and follower of John Calvin, he served as pastor to a group of English exiles. His Scottish friends invited him to come back to his native land and lead a reformation of the Church in 1555 but, once there, he saw that the time was not yet right and he returned to Switzerland. By 1559 the situation had changed, and on 2 May he landed at Leith. Nine days later he preached in St John's Kirk, Perth – and a riot followed, with the local people breaking down the statues in the church and in the town's friaries. The Reformation had begun.

Knox did not carry through the Reformation single-handed, as people used to believe. The dramatic changes were led by the nobles, but Knox played a vital part, motivating their followers with his eloquent preaching, his biting humour and his force of personality. As time went, on the Protestant lords came to the conclusion that he was too honest, outspoken and tactless to represent them in their diplomatic negotiations with their potential English allies. Nonetheless, Knox's continuing importance should not be underplayed. So was he also a woman-hater? Many have thought so because he called his most notorious book *The First Blast of the Trumpet against the Monstrous Regiment of Women*. However, the title is usually misunderstood. If it is translated into modern English, it becomes *The First Blast of the Trumpet against the Unnatural Rule of Women*, which is something rather different. Knox had dreadful memories of Mary Tudor's persecution of his Protestant friends in England, and that was what had inspired the book. Apart from that, his views about gender were typical of his time and, when he argued that women were frail and fickle, he was simply repeating what many other authors had said.

In spite of these opinions, Knox was throughout his career a sympathetic and understanding counsellor of troubled parishioners. As many ministers do, he had a devoted following among the women of his congregation, and he was endlessly patient with those who had recently converted but were worried about whether they had done the right thing. In private life he had been happily married and, if he had been in his thirties before finding a wife, that was because, as a priest, he had been obliged to remain celibate. He had never shown any signs of looking for an illicit partner, as many of the Catholic clergy had done, and, in the end, it was a member of his English congregation who had urged him to take a wife. He was overworked and exhausted, and

Elizabeth Bowes, wife of the captain of Norham Castle, had suggested that one of her own daughters, Marjorie, would be the ideal person. She had been carefully educated, she could read and write, and she would be a great help to him with all his paperwork. This proved to be so. They were happy together, they had two sons during their Swiss exile, and Calvin thought her a most delightful person. Sadly, Marjorie died of an unknown illness in the winter of 1560, the year after they settled in Edinburgh. When Knox remarried three years later, he once again enjoyed a satisfactory domestic life with his new wife Margaret Stewart and their three small girls. In short, he was normally on good terms with women, but the Reformed faith remained his greatest passion in life.

Did Mary, Queen of Scots feel as strongly about her religion? She was brought up at a time and in a place where most people accepted Roman Catholicism as a natural fact of life. Indeed, her relatives were prominent in the Church. A great-uncle and her favourite uncle were cardinals, her father had led the fight against Lutherans on the French borders, her grandmother kept a coffin near her apartments to remind herself that life is fleeting, and her young aunts were destined to become abbesses. Like her mother and her grandmother, Mary had throughout her life an unwavering attachment to the Roman Catholic Church. This did not mean that she was oblivious to the rise of Protestantism during her French years. One of the childhood exercises set by her tutor had been for her to compose letters to John Calvin about his controversial writings, and, as the young bride of François II, she had been staying in the Castle of Amboise when Protestant plotters against the Guise family were publicly hanged just outside, as a terrible warning to any who thought to follow them.

Always an avid reader, Mary had in her library in Scotland books on both sides of the religious controversy, from those written by René Benoist, her own confessor, in the early 1560s, to at least one work by Martin Luther. Like a group of French thinkers who included her first mother-in-law Catherine de Medici, she believed that civil disorder was to be avoided at all costs and, if this meant tolerating Protestantism in the short term, so be it. When she first came to Scotland, the policy of toleration was forced upon her by circumstances, and the later traumas of her personal rule would mean that she would even turn to the Reformed Church for support, but none of that altered her personal faith.

Given their very different backgrounds, it was all but inevitable that Mary and Knox would clash. If his account of events is correct, she opened her first conversation with him that late summer day in Holyroodhouse by demanding to know why he had stirred up rebellion against her mother and herself and written that seditious book, *The First Blast of the Trumpet*. She had even heard that he dabbled in necromancy, she said, meaning black magic. In reply, Knox defended his theory that the people had the right to overthrow an ungodly monarch. Just as children had the right to imprison their father if he tried to kill them, he said, so were the subjects of a country justified in imprisoning a monarch who tried to murder the children of God.

According to Knox, Mary was at a loss when she heard what he had to say and stood dumbfounded for a quarter of an hour – no doubt something of an exaggeration. Eventually she replied, with her famous irony. Were her subjects to obey him and not her, and should they do what they pleased and not what she commanded? Was she to be subject to them instead of them being subject to her? The debate then took a more theological turn, with Knox telling her that the Reformers condemned the mass because it was the invention of man and had nothing to do with the scriptures. He cited many Biblical references and, in the end, Mary could only sigh and wish aloud that some of the Roman Catholic clergy were there too, for they could have answered him better than she could do. The conversation ended on that note.

According to Knox's history, he and Mary had four more private meetings, three of them confrontational and one of them almost amicable. In December 1562 he was summoned once more to Holyroodhouse for publicly criticising the queen's fondness for dancing. When she accused him passionately of turning her subjects against her, he retorted that he had been quoted out of context. Realising that the rumours she had heard had been exaggerated, she took a more placatory tone and urged him to come and tell her if she did something he disliked. He replied tersely that he had no time to rebuke individuals, but she was welcome to ask for a meeting with him or come to his public sermons. Despite the nineteenth-century paintings of Mary being harangued in church, that never happened, for, of course, she would never have attended a Protestant service. Meanwhile, Knox's manner was hardly that of a subject addressing a monarch and she was irritated to say the least.

The third time they met was when she complained to him about some priests in the west of Scotland being arrested for saying mass. He replied that they had been dealt with according to the laws of Scotland, which was true. To his surprise, she saw him again the following morning and was in a much more conciliatory mood, asking him to mediate in the marriage difficulties of her half-sister the Countess of Argyll, as he had done once before. Probably after advice from her Protestant half-brother the Earl of Moray, she was trying to establish a better relationship with Knox and the conversation was almost friendly, but they were soon at odds again over the prospect of Mary's own marriage. Knox feared that she was about to choose a foreign Roman Catholic prince, with disastrous consequences for the Scottish Church. She was furious at his interference, he lost his temper, and she was reduced to tears of rage by his savage retorts. She sent him away and never again did they have a private meeting.

During the later dramatic troubles of Mary's reign, Knox withdrew to stay with his first wife's relatives in the north of England, but ten days after the queen surrendered to her Protestant lords and was imprisoned in Lochleven Castle, he was back in Scotland. For the rest of his life, he preached vehemently against her, demanding her execution for the crimes of adultery and murder. Mary's efforts to conciliate him had been fruitless. Apart from his dislike of many of the doctrines of the Roman Catholic Church, the burning of his mentor George Wishart and the persecution of his English Protestant friends under Mary I had given him such an intense loathing of Catholicism that he was unable to see Mary, Queen of Scots as an individual. She was quite simply

Chapter 4

Was it love at first sight for Mary and Lord Darnley?

MYTH

Mary, Queen of Scots met Lord Darnley for the first time in the spring of 1565 and instantly fell in love with him because he was young, tall and handsome. She forgot about all her far more important suitors and married him within weeks, without a thought for any political concerns.

FACTS

Mary, Queen of Scots had spent Christmas 1564 in Holyroodhouse, but at the end of January she travelled to St Andrews, where she stayed for about a fortnight. In mid-February she set off for Edinburgh once more, riding with her retinue along the south coast of Fife. In those days, any royal court was frequently on the move. A king or queen was always accompanied by a large number of courtiers and servants. If the journey was a long one, they would visit some member of the local aristocracy who had premises large enough to accommodate them. There they would stay for a few days or a few weeks, eating the local produce. When it was exhausted they would move on, and the building would be cleaned and put back to normal use. Demanding as this was, it was regarded as a great honour by their host. In fact, many of the nobility kept a special monarch's room hoping, often in vain, for just such a royal visitation.

On 17 February 1565 Mary was staying at Wemyss, in the large, medieval cliff-top castle overlooking the estuary of the River Forth, and it was there that Lord Darnley sought her out. He would have arrived with his own attendants, and when he explained that he was the Earl of Lennox's son, he would have been granted an audience with the queen. What followed was not, however, a case of love at first sight, nor was this a spontaneous encounter. The young couple had already met twice before and, as on the two previous occasions, their coming together had been carefully planned by Lord Darnley's mother, who was also Mary's aunt. In other words, Mary and Darnley were first cousins.

In order to understand the connection, we must look back again to the Tudor family tree. As we have seen, Henry VIII had two sisters. The elder, Princess Margaret, had married James IV, King of Scots and when he was killed at the Battle of Flodden in 1513, their small son became King James V. That was not the end of married life for her, however. By nature, Queen Margaret was impetuous, and she then embarked on what can only be described as a chaotic marital career. She fell in love with Archibald, Earl of Angus, a handsome, 19-year-old widower and married him secretly less than a year after her husband's death. They had a daughter, whom she called after herself. Before long, Queen Margaret fell out with Angus and divorced him, married Henry, Lord Methven instead, and then tried unsuccessfully to divorce him so that she could remarry Angus.

While all this was going on, her little daughter, Lady Margaret Douglas, was being brought up in England. What had happened was that, during one of her parents' violent quarrels, Angus had snatched her from her mother's arms and ridden off with her. Over the next few years, he took her with him to France and then moved to England. It was hardly a stable background for the child, although Angus no doubt employed nurses and women servants to look after her, and he eventually agreed that she should go and live in the household of her cousin, Princess Mary, daughter of Henry VIII and Catherine of Aragon. There, she was brought up as a devout Catholic and her sparkling personality soon made her a favourite with the English royal family. Princess Mary was her close friend and her uncle Henry VIII treated her indulgently. When she was old enough, she became a lady-in-waiting to his rapidly changing succession of wives.

Lady Margaret seems to have been flirtatious, too, and had not a little of her mother's recklessness. At one point she became secretly engaged to Anne Boleyn's uncle, Thomas Howard, and, when Henry VIII found out, he imprisoned her for a time in the Tower of London. In spite of this, she then had an affair with Charles Howard, the brother of Henry's fifth wife Katherine Howard. This time, the King placed her under house arrest and sent his chief minister, Thomas Cromwell, to warn her to beware of making a third mistake. Henry was actually being rather tolerant. Margaret knew perfectly well that, as a member of the royal family, she had to have his permission to marry, and that he would choose her bridegroom. The trouble was that he showed no signs of doing so.

Monarchs were deeply suspicious of their close relatives, always fearing that they might try to seize the throne for themselves. History was full of examples of this happening. Female relatives were as much of a danger as men because, left to themselves, they might marry an ambitious husband who could try to depose the king in her name. For Margaret, this was all rather frustrating, and not simply because she was deprived of marrying a man she loved. She could normally have expected to have been provided with a husband by the time she was 16 or 17, the usual age for marriage in those days but, when she was in her mid-twenties, she was still single and her uncle showed no sign of finding her a partner.

In the end, Henry VIII did marry her off, for political reasons of course. One of his ambitions was to rule Scotland as well as England, so that he could end Scotland's alliance with his enemy, France, and he was always looking for Scots who would be suitable instruments for this policy. After the fiasco of the cancelled marriage between his son Prince Edward and Mary, Queen of Scots, he wanted to build up a body of Scottish supporters, and he decided that Matthew, Earl of Lennox would suit his purposes. Lennox was living at the Scottish court, but he was in a rebellious mood. He had been brought up by relatives who had settled in France, but he had been lured back to Scotland with promises that the widowed Mary of Guise might marry him. He was a significant figure, because he was descended from one of the daughters of James II, but he had a great rival in the Earl of

Arran, who had a similar and slightly more senior claim to the throne and was, of course, the Scottish regent. To make matters worse, Mary of Guise made it clear that she had no intention of taking another husband. As a result, Lennox was ready to listen to Henry's approaches. However, he demanded something in return for his support. He wanted to marry one of Henry's relatives. The king was not willing to give him one of his own daughters and so, instead, Lennox asked for Henry's niece, Lady Margaret Douglas.

Henry was wary, for the usual reasons, but in the end he agreed. Assured of a welcome, Lennox fled to England. With his French upbringing, he was a handsome, sophisticated figure and, when he met Lady Margaret, the two fell in love. They were married at St James's Palace in London on 6 July 1544, in the presence of Henry VIII himself. On his wedding day, Lennox became a naturalised Englishman. He subsequently forfeited his Scottish estates when he tried to further Henry's policies with regard to Scotland, but he and his bride were compensated with properties in London and in Yorkshire. Also, Henry allegedly told the new Countess of Lennox that, should his own children die, he would be happy for hers to succeed to the English throne. If he really said this, it was a remark she never forgot. During the next twelve years, she and Lennox had eight children, only two of whom survived. The elder was Henry, Lord Darnley, born on 7 December 1545 and called after his great-uncle Henry VIII.

For personal reasons, it was hardly surprising that Lady Lennox set such store by her elder son, but she had wider ambitions too. Through his father, Darnley had a strong claim to the Scottish throne if anything should happen to little Mary, Queen of Scots, and through herself he could even hope to inherit the English throne. Other candidates might stand in the way but, as Lady Lennox was painfully aware, life expectancy was short, and monarchs and their heirs could all too easily perish in this age of battle, murder and sudden death. Meanwhile, she would do everything she could to keep her adored elder son at the forefront of affairs.

Lord Darnley must, of course, have an education which would allow him to cut a fine figure at the royal courts of England and Scotland. His mother therefore made sure that he grew up speaking Scots, English, French and Latin, which was still the international spoken language of diplomacy. Fortunately he was healthy, and when he was in his teens he grew tall and strong. He was a fine horseman, and he loved hunting and falconry. His handwriting was unusually regular and elegant, and he was musical. He was an accomplished player on the lute, and he could sing and dance. It was awkward when the Protestant Edward VI succeeded his father, and the devoutly Roman Catholic Lennox family found it best to stay at Temple Newsam on their Yorkshire estate rather than being able to live in London. Lady Lennox was undeterred however, and, thanks to her activities, their Yorkshire home became a centre for Catholic conspiracy in England.

With her network of spies, she would have known about the onset of Edward VI's tuberculosis and, when he died in the summer of 1553 and her old friend Princess Mary became Queen Mary I of England, she rejoiced. Not only would Catholicism be restored, but also Mary was already 37 years old and still unmarried. Surely she would be willing to recognise either Lady Lennox or her charming elder son as her heir? After all, the other most obvious claimant was Mary I's half-sister Elizabeth, and it was well known that not only was she a Protestant, but the sisters had never been on good terms. Lady Lennox and her family therefore hurried to London and the new queen welcomed them gladly, showering them with gifts and giving them apartments in the Palace of Westminster. Lennox was made Master of the Hawks and young Lord Darnley received three suits of fine clothing and Edward VI's lutes. Even when Mary married Philip II of Spain in Winchester Cathedral the following year, Lady Lennox was not dismayed. She helped to carry the queen's train that day and joined in the celebrations afterwards, secure in the knowledge that her friend was almost too old for child-bearing.

It was probably in this context that his proud parents, the following year, commissioned a portrait of Darnley from the leading court painter, Hans Eworth. It shows a round-faced, fair-haired boy with an innocent expression, wearing highly fashionable black clothes. Mary I never did recognise Darnley as her heir, however, and when she died in 1558, the throne went to her half-sister Elizabeth after all. Furious, Lady Lennox lost no time in making it known that she herself was the rightful queen. Unlike Elizabeth, she was legitimate. Elizabeth responded by ordering her lawyers to prove that, because Lady Lennox's parents had later divorced, it was she who was illegitimate. In spite of this bad beginning, Lady Lennox saw that she would be better to cultivate Elizabeth's favour, and somehow she did indeed become friendly with the queen. Although Elizabeth was only 25, she showed no signs of marrying, and there was still hope that the English crown might one day pass to a member of the Lennox family. At the same time, Lady Lennox's attention turned to what was happening in France.

Her niece Mary, Queen of Scots had married the Dauphin François that same summer, but everyone knew that he was delicate and, if he did not survive, then Mary would need a new husband. Indeed, the thought of a marriage between Mary and Darnley seems to have been at the back of Lady Lennox's mind from the start, and now that the English situation had become so difficult, it might be a more achievable goal. When Henri II died in 1559, Lady Lennox decided to send her congratulations to the new monarch and his wife by a very special messenger. Darnley was only 13, too young to be sent on an important mission alone, and so he was dispatched to France with his tutor John Elder. They were to travel in the strictest secrecy and, when he was shown into the royal presence, Darnley was to present a letter from his father asking for Lennox's estates to be restored to him.

The boy was indeed allowed an audience with Mary, Queen of Scots, who rejected his father's petition but was kind to Darnley himself, inviting him to attend her husband's coronation and making him a gift of 1,000 gold coins. That seemed a good sign, and then, in November 1560, Lady Lennox heard some very exciting news. François II was dead and her niece was a widow, a very eligible widow. She immediately sent Darnley to France again to offer the family's condolences, seeing this as a wonderful opportunity for him. As soon as her spies told her that Mary was thinking of returning to Scotland, she began her vigorous campaign, or so Mary would tell Elizabeth I in later years. Lady Lennox bombarded Mary with messages, letters and gifts, urging her to marry Lord Darnley. He would make the ideal husband, she said, for like Mary he was descended from both the Stewart and the Tudor kings, and his claim to the English throne would strengthen hers. What was more, he had been brought up as a Catholic and he would always be a respectful husband.

Mary later declared that she had not until that point given a thought to either Darnley or his mother, because she had many other much more high-born suitors in mind. That was almost certainly true. Ignoring her lack of response, Lady Lennox continued her campaign by telling her friends that her son was to marry Mary. In fact, she became so over-excited that she even said that the young couple would replace Elizabeth I on the English throne. Needless to say, when Elizabeth got to hear of that, she was furious, threw Lord Lennox into the Tower of London and placed Lady Lennox under house arrest. Lord Darnley managed to escape to the continent. His father had relatives in Aubigny, and he presumably stayed with them, usefully improving his French.

Realising that she had gone too far, Lady Lennox set about ingratiating herself once more with Elizabeth and, against all the odds, she succeeded. Lord Darnley was allowed back and in July 1563 an eye-witness reported that he was at the court in London every day, often playing the lute for the queen.

When Elizabeth went on her usual summer progress through the countryside, Darnley and his parents were in her retinue, and she was even persuaded to agree that Lord Lennox could go back to Scotland to try to reclaim his estates in person. However, she changed her mind when some of her Scottish allies warned her that, while he was there, he was sure to try to arrange a marriage between his son and Mary, Queen of Scots. His journey was postponed, but Lady Lennox went to work on Elizabeth again, and he was finally allowed to go to Edinburgh in September 1564. Thinking to please Elizabeth, Mary gave Lennox back his earldom.

The following month, Darnley was so much in favour with Elizabeth I that he was allowed to carry the sword of state in front of her when she gave her favourite, Robert Dudley, the earldom of Leicester. The English queen was at that time engaged in a policy of suggesting various inherently unsuitable husbands for Mary, Queen of Scots, largely in an attempt to prevent her from marrying at all. She had insultingly offered Leicester as a possibility, despite the fact that, according to rumour, he was her own lover. Now, during the ceremony, the queen asked the Scottish ambassador Sir James Melville what he thought of Leicester. He made a diplomatic reply, but she then remarked that perhaps he preferred the tall lad at the other side of the room, pointing to Darnley. Melville retorted sharply that no woman of any spirit would choose Darnley, for he was clean-shaven, unlike his contemporaries, and 'lady-faced'. He had probably heard rumours that Darnley was bisexual.

Melville might have found Elizabeth I difficult, but he liked Lady Lennox and, when he was returning to Scotland, she persuaded him to take various gifts to her friends. These included an expensive diamond ring, a clock, an ornamental mirror and a very impressive brooch for Mary, Queen of Scots. Shortly afterwards, she somehow managed to cajole Elizabeth into saying that Darnley could join his father in Scotland for a period of three months. That is how the young man came to arrive at Wemyss Castle one early spring day in 1565. It was an entirely calculated encounter.

So what was Mary's reaction when she saw her cousin again? Melville, who was there, claimed afterwards that Mary was favourably impressed with Lord Darnley, declaring him to be the best-proportioned tall man that she had ever seen. However, historians are agreed that there was at first no sign that Mary had fallen in love with him. She still had lingering thoughts of the Spanish marriage but, as the weeks went by, her hopes of Don Carlos were finally ended, and her cousin proved an agreeable companion, eager to please and a welcome contrast to the belligerent Scottish lords. When he fell ill with a bad cold and then measles, she nursed him tenderly, spending hours at his bedside.

It was only then that Mary began seriously to consider him as a possible husband. Even so, sexual attraction was far from being the only consideration. It was true that widows had far more freedom of choice in the selection of a husband than single women did, but, for a queen in her own right, it was a different matter. Everyone seemed to have an opinion about who the bridegroom should be. The Earl of Moray, her other statesmen, John Knox, her relatives and friends and, most importantly, Elizabeth I all thought that they had the right to tell her what to do. In most cases, Mary reacted with annoyance at what she saw as their interference, but she was eager to cultivate Elizabeth's friendship, and surely, by allowing Darnley to come to Scotland, the English queen was giving a signal that she thought he would make a good consort. If Mary married Darnley, she would be combining her claim to the throne of England with his, and giving Elizabeth a double reason to recognise Mary as her heir, or so Mary thought.

In fact, Elizabeth was already regretting having allowed Darnley to travel north. In mid-May, Mary learned that she was totally opposed to the marriage. Angry and disillusioned at this further example of Elizabeth's duplicitous behaviour, Mary immediately made Darnley Earl of Ross. This was taken as a sign that a royal engagement would follow. When she heard the news, Elizabeth furiously recalled both Darnley and his father to London, but they ignored her orders and, on 29 July 1565, Mary and Darnley were married in her private chapel in the Palace of Holyroodhouse.

Chapter 5

Did Mary have an affair with David Rizzio?

MYTH

Not long after she married Lord Darnley, Mary, Queen of Scots began an affair with David Rizzio, an Italian musician in her household. She ignored her husband, and it was Rizzio who was the real father of her only child, the future King James VI and I.

FACTS

Mary, Queen of Scots and her new husband, Lord Darnley, were happy together at first, but it was not long before jealous Scottish noblemen began to make trouble between them. The Cardinal of Lorraine, Mary's uncle, had written Darnley off as being no more than an agreeable young fool when he had met him in France and indeed her bridegroom soon proved to be immature and gullible. When Mary's enemies whispered to him that she was far too friendly with a member of her household, he believed them and was consumed with jealousy. But was Mary really having an affair with an Italian singer named David Rizzio?

Rizzio was nine or ten years older than the queen, born about 1533 in the small village of Pancalieri, about twenty miles south of Turin. It lay in the duchy of Savoy, and it seems that several members of the Rizzio family had worked for the duke. Rizzio inherited his musical talents from his father, who was an impoverished musician, and he himself became a fine singer and an accomplished lute-player. He may have had a university education, and he certainly found employment with the influential Cardinal Cesare Usdimo, the Archbishop of Turin, who appreciated his abilities and took an interest in his career. The cardinal came from an aristocratic family and, in 1561, one of his relatives, Robertino Solarto, Marquis of Moretto, was sent off by the Duke of Savoy on a diplomatic mission to Scotland.

That was the year when Mary, Queen of Scots returned from France. During the months that followed, foreign ambassadors made their way to Scotland to see the newly returned queen for themselves and gauge her abilities. Moretto had special instructions. He was to say that he had come to persuade Mary to send a representative to the ecclesiastical Council of Trent, which had been meeting off and on since 1545 in an effort to introduce reforms into the Roman Catholic Church and stamp out heresies. He also had secret instructions, for he had been told to further the cause of one of Mary's many suitors, Alfonso d'Este, Duke of Ferrara. Moretto arrived in Edinburgh in December 1561 and in his retinue, acting as one of his secretaries, was David Rizzio, recommended to him by his relative Cardinal Usdimo.

It seems that the Marquis of Moretto urged the ambitious Rizzio to find employment at the Scottish court. Mary, Queen of Scots was known to be very fond of music and, soon after his arrival, Rizzio got to hear that she was looking for someone with a good bass voice to make up her quartet of French singers. They sang sacred music for her in her Chapel Royal, and they also entertained her in her apartments with secular songs. Rizzio was staying in the Palace of Holyroodhouse, although in very humble circumstances. He was not even provided with a bed, sleeping at night under a couple of rugs on top of an old chest in a passageway, but it was worth it to be on the fringes of court life. He made himself agreeable to the three choristers and pressed them to let him sing with them in the queen's presence. He did this twice, and she liked his deep, powerful voice.

Meanwhile, his employer was proving less successful. The Marquis of Moretto stayed in Scotland for several weeks, but the Duke of Ferrara was not nearly important enough to be a serious contender for Mary's hand, and her advisers convinced her that it would not be a good idea for her to send a representative to the Council of Trent from newly Protestant Scotland. There was nothing more the Marquis could do, and so he left for home. Before he did so, however, he recommended Rizzio for a permanent position in the royal household, and Mary employed him as one of her *valets de chambre*. On 8 January 1562 he was paid £50 Scots for his services. Singing did not occupy all his time, and he was also given responsibility for domestic duties such as looking after the bedding of the royal household and supplying liveries for the pages and some of the other servants.

The various foreigners who formed part of the queen's household were unwelcome to many of the Scots, who were quick to sneer that Rizzio was old (he was about 30, but the other choristers may have been younger), small, ugly and even deformed. We cannot judge for ourselves, for no authentic portrait of him exists, but his talents and his personality made up for any defects in his appearance. Sir James Melville thought him a merry fellow and a good musician, and he soon became a great favourite with the queen. He spoke French, he knew all the gossip of the French court and he was lively and amusing.

Three years after Rizzio's arrival in Scotland, Mary dismissed one of her secretaries, Augustine Raullet, who was suspected of spying for the English. He had looked after her voluminous French correspondence, and it must have seemed to her that Rizzio was the obvious man to replace him. He could write as well as speak French, he was fluent in Italian and Latin and, after all, he had been one of the Marquis of Moretto's secretaries, so he had the necessary experience. He continued his singing, kept on some of his former activities as a *valet de chambre*, and his secretarial duties meant that he spent long hours in Mary's company. It seemed to the jealous nobles that he was always at her elbow during the day, advising her about what to say to her correspondents, and he would sit playing cards with her until the early hours of the morning. The humble David the Singer had been transformed into Seigneur Davie, someone who strutted around in elaborate clothes, rode out on the best horses and had to be bribed by those who wished to gain the queen's

taken up with royal business for a good deal of the time, whereas he thought they should spend their days enjoying themselves. His false friends were quick to point out that, although he was now known as King Henry, Mary had not yet given him the crown matrimonial. In other words, he was a consort but not a joint monarch, sharing his wife's powers. It was an easy matter to arouse his resentment about that, and they also began to whisper in his ear that Mary was being unfaithful to him. Had he not noticed that she and David Rizzio were very friendly? When it became known that the queen was pregnant, they seized their opportunity and asked Darnley if he was sure that the coming baby was really his. Darnley, at first huffy and petulant, was now seething with discontent, and Mary's enemies finalised their plans.

By mid-February 1566, the English ambassador Thomas Randolph was able to tell Elizabeth I's advisers that there was a conspiracy to murder David Rizzio and make Darnley king in reality, not merely in name. On 1 March, Darnley signed a sinister bond, a document declaring that he intended to rid Scotland of those who had taken advantage of the queen's kindness, especially the Italian called David. It could well be that Rizzio would be killed, the bond said, and very possibly in the presence of the queen herself. The significance of this last phrase is that the conspirators may have hoped that this violent attack would cause Mary to miscarry or even die of the shock. Another significant figure was also involved. Mary's half-brother, Lord James Stewart, now Earl of Moray, had bitterly opposed the Darnley marriage and had been displaced as her principal adviser. He had raised a rebellion against her and then fled to England. Now he and his allies signed their own document, promising that they would support the scheme and make sure that Darnley was rewarded with the crown matrimonial.

They had their own agenda, of course. The next session of the Scottish parliament would open on 7 March, and it was expected that a bill of attainder against Moray would be passed, authorising all his Scottish possessions to be seized as a punishment for his rebellion. He was determined that this would never happen. Mary opened parliament, as planned, and it was arranged that the bill of attainder would be passed on 12 March. However, on the evening of 9 March, the conspirators struck. The queen was six months pregnant now. She was staying in her apartments at the Palace of Holyroodhouse, and she was in the habit of having supper in the little room leading from her bedchamber. It can still be seen today, and it is a very small apartment, with space for only a table, perhaps a bench and a few chairs. With her were two of her close relatives: her half-brother Lord Robert Stewart and her half-sister Jean, Countess of Argyll. Both were the illegitimate children of James V. Also present were several members of her household. David Rizzio was there, and so was her French apothecary along with Robert Beaton, the Master of her Household, Arthur Erskine, Captain of the Guard, and a couple of domestic servants.

Mary sat at the side of the table, with the countess at one end and Rizzio at the other. A candlestick, probably a small candelabrum, had been placed in the middle of the table. Scarcely had the meal begun when there was a sudden and unexpected noise close by. In keeping with the usual royal custom, the King of Scots normally had his apartments on the first floor, with his queen's immediately above. In this instance, Mary, although the monarch, had chosen to occupy the upstairs suite, which had been used by her mother, and so Darnley was downstairs in the king's chambers. There was a narrow communicating stone stair between them in the thickness of the wall. Someone was now coming up that stair. The tapestry concealing its entrance was swept aside and there in the doorway stood Lord Darnley himself. This was surprising. He had given up any effort to spend his evenings with the queen, and, according to widely circulated reports, preferred to roam about the town, drinking and visiting prostitutes. But here he was, and looking uncharacteristically cheerful.

Seating himself beside Mary, he placed his arm round her waist. Surprised, she spoke to him, presumably asking him what he wanted, but they had time to say only a few words to each other before there was a loud clattering on the stair and another figure appeared, a man in full armour, his face ghastly pale. It was Lord Ruthven, who had been ill for months and who had been reported to be near death only a few days before. In a voice of doom, he ordered the queen to give up Rizzio to him. At this, Mary rounded furiously on her husband, demanding to know what he had to do with all of this, to which Darnley replied defiantly that he knew nothing about what was happening. Turning away in disgust, the queen ordered Ruthven to leave at once or be condemned as a traitor. If Rizzio had committed any offence, she said, she would punish him legally.

Ruthven ignored her, Mary rose to her feet in alarm, Darnley seized her and the terrified Rizzio dived behind her, cowering in a window embrasure and clinging to the pleats on the back of her gown. At the same time, the Captain of the Guard and the other men in the room leapt forward to try to seize Ruthven, but he brandished a pistol at them and they fell back. At that moment, a group of men rushed into the queen's audience chamber from the main staircase and charged through into the supper room. The supper table was overturned, plates and cups fell to the floor, and the quick-thinking Countess of Argyll snatched up the candlestick before it too fell and plunged them all into darkness. One of the intruders threateningly put a pistol to the queen's stomach and Lord Ruthven hauled Rizzio out into her bedchamber. George Douglas, Darnley's uncle, promptly seized Darnley's dagger and thrust it into the Italian, who was screaming: 'Justice! Justice! Save me, Madame, save me!'

She could do nothing, and he was dragged through her bedchamber and out into her audience chamber, the conspirators stabbing him with their daggers until, on Darnley's orders, his body was hurled down the main staircase and thrown across the very chest he had first used as a bed in the Palace of Holyroodhouse. Fifty-six wounds were found on his body. In the aftermath, held prisoner by the intruders, Mary wept, asking over and over again what had happened to Rizzio. Much later, one of her ladies was allowed to come to her. She had seen David's body, and broke the news of his death. At that, according to her own account, Mary dried her eyes, declaring that she would shed no more tears. Instead, she would plan her revenge. As for Darnley, when she spoke to him, reproaching him for this dreadful occurrence, he merely replied with a torrent of childishly jealous accusations about how his wife had been ignoring him. She never came to his chamber as she used to do and, if he came to her apartments, Davie was always there.

Rizzio's body was hastily interred in a graveyard near Holyroodhouse. According to some accounts, the queen later had it removed and buried in her own Chapel Royal at the palace, although he is also reputed to lie in the cemetery of the Canongate Church. By her own resourcefulness, Mary managed to escape from her captors, taking Darnley with her and, on 19 June that year, she safely gave birth to a son, the future James VI. When Darnley came to see the baby after the birth, Mary made a point of telling him, in front of others, that this was his son and not the child of any other man, adding bitterly that the prince was so much Darnley's own son that she feared it would be the worse for him in later life.

Was Mary speaking the truth, or had she and Rizzio been lovers? Historians, even those openly hostile to Mary, are agreed that there was never any sexual relationship between the two. Gossip and rumour always circulated in the overheated atmosphere of royal courts, and this story would never have been believed had it not been for Darnley's jealous insecurity and the sinister opportunism of the queen's enemies. Mary was always kind-hearted and forthcoming with people, but from her earliest days she had been brought up to remember that she was a monarch, and she preserved a regal distance between herself and even her most favoured friends. Lonely and longing for the sort of company she had enjoyed in France, she appreciated Rizzio's quick wit and his musical abilities. However, he remained what he was, her loyal and appreciated servant, but nothing more.

Chapter 6

Did Mary murder Lord Darnley?

MYTH

In 1567, Lord Darnley, the second husband of Mary, Queen of Scots, was killed in an explosion when Kirk o' Field, the house where he was staying, was blown up. So many people hated Darnley that there were different groups of conspirators lurking about that night. However, Mary and her lover, the Earl of Bothwell, were the guilty parties. She had lured Darnley to Kirk o' Field so that Bothwell could kill him. As soon as her husband was dead, she rejoiced and began planning her wedding to Bothwell.

FACTS

It is true that Lord Darnley died at Kirk o' Field on 10 February 1567, but he was not killed by the explosion. So what actually happened? It is possible to piece together the evidence from witness statements by people who were there, Mary's own account of events and reports from foreign ambassadors. At about two o'clock in the morning, Edinburgh was shaken by a deafening explosion which seemed to come from the south-east of the town. People in the area leapt from their beds in alarm and rushed out into the street to see what was happening, some without even waiting to put on any clothes. Mary, Queen of Scots was in her bedchamber in her Palace of Holyroodhouse and of course, like everyone else, she was wakened by the noise. Bewildered and still half-asleep, she thought that cannon were firing, and she asked her ladies-in-waiting what was happening. Was the town being attacked?

James, 4th Earl of Bothwell, who was sheriff of Edinburgh, was one of the courtiers spending the night in the palace. He appeared, took charge and sent messengers to find out what was going on before climbing up the hill to Kirk o' Field himself. It was pitch dark, of course, but by the light of torches it was possible to glimpse the scene of devastation. Kirk o' Field stood just inside the town wall, on the site of the present Old College of Edinburgh University. In those days, it consisted of a residential square. On two sides there were small stone houses with crow-step gables, and on the third side was an imposing mansion belonging to the Hamilton family. It was presently occupied by John Hamilton, the Roman Catholic Archbishop of St Andrews. On the fourth side, close to the town wall, were more small, gabled houses alongside a larger one, called the Old Provost's Lodging. Now all that remained of it were piles of masonry and timber. It had been completely demolished. The sight was all the more horrifying because everyone knew that not only had Lord Darnley been staying there, but the queen herself had spent a couple of nights in the Lodging recently, occupying the bedchamber below his.

Word soon came that Mary was safe, but what about her husband? Rescuers dug frantically among the rubble, but no trace of him could be found. It was only when daylight came that his fate was revealed. The Old Provost's Lodging had its own garden, but beyond that and over the town wall was another large grassy area. There, the searchers came upon a macabre scene. The body of Lord Darnley lay beneath a tree, wearing only his nightshirt. A few metres away lay his valet, William Taylor, also dead. Near them, neatly arranged, were a doublet, a cloak, a wooden chair and a dagger. A shout went up, a large crowd gathered, and the townspeople gazed at the corpses in disbelief until Bothwell came and ordered them away.

The bodies bore no signs of violence. There were no knife wounds or gunshot wounds, no bruising and apparently no signs of strangulation. In a sketch of the scene, sent to Sir William Cecil in London shortly afterwards, Darnley's head seems to lie at an odd angle against his right shoulder, but there was no contemporary suggestion that his neck had been broken. He had obviously not perished in the explosion, for his corpse showed no signs of scorching. It seemed that he and Taylor had been smothered or strangled as they tried to escape from the house. They must have heard something that alarmed them – perhaps the doors being locked from the outside, muffled voices, or the men with the gunpowder stumbling about in the downstairs bedchamber used by the queen.

The doublet and cloak were easily enough explained. Presumably they had been taken so that Darnley could put them on over his nightshirt. As for the chair, Mary's recent biographer John Guy has explained the usual means of escape from the upper storey of a burning house. Ropes would be tied to a chair, which was then, with its occupant, lowered down to ground level. If Darnley had come out at a first-floor window overlooking the town wall, then he would have been sixteen feet above the ground, and so this may well have been the method used.

It seems that he was then intercepted by a group of men deliberately posted at the back of the house. The Marquis of Moretto, Rizzio's old employer, was in Edinburgh at the time, and he found out that women who lived in a couple of nearby cottages had heard Darnley scream: 'Oh my kinsmen, have mercy upon me, for the love of Him who had mercy on all the world.' This suggests that the men who took him were members of the Douglas family, relatives of his mother. The women also spoke of seeing thirteen men hurrying along a lane at the back, but only eleven returning. The Douglases and their friends had seemingly dragged Darnley away, strangled him and the valet, and dumped their bodies in the large garden. The presence of these other plotters was no random accident, and the latest historical thinking is that, far from different conspirators rushing about in confusion, they had all been part of a deliberate plan to make sure that Darnley did not escape should something go wrong with the gunpowder plot.

Later interrogation of witnesses showed that Sir James Balfour, brother of Robert Balfour, the owner of the Old Provost's Lodging, had supplied the gunpowder for the explosion in very large quantities. Presumably the conspirators were trying to make sure that the house was completely demolished, in order to destroy any evidence of their crime. Sir James Balfour had possibly stored it initially in the house next door, which he owned. Bothwell and his men had been responsible for deploying it in the cellars and in the lower bedchamber. According to one witness, it was Bothwell who lit the long trail of powder which formed the fuse, and then was so impatient for it to go off that he hurried forward to see how it was progressing. One of his companions pulled him away in the nick of time, seconds before there was a blinding flash and then the tremendous noise of the explosion.

Bothwell was obviously deeply implicated in all that happened that night, but what about the queen? Does her reaction to the explosion suggest that she was guilty or innocent of the crime? She was reported to be deeply shaken when Bothwell brought her the news of Darnley's death, and she was left in great fear of her life, convinced that her own death had also been intended. In her account of events, she described how she had spent the evening with Darnley at Kirk o' Field and would almost certainly have slept in the house had not someone reminded her that she had promised to attend that evening's wedding celebrations for one of her favourite servants, Bastian Pages. If God had not intervened and prompted her to go to the wedding party, she said much later, she would have been killed and the conspirators would then have gone down to Holyroodhouse, seized her baby son and ruled Scotland in his name.

Now she put on deepest mourning and shut herself in the traditional darkened room. She gave orders for her husband's body to be embalmed and, for three days, it lay in state in her

Chapel Royal at Holyrood. Her lords insisted that she go and look at the corpse. She stood gazing at her dead husband for a long time in complete silence. Usually, her emotions were near the surface and she wept easily, but now she seemed to be in deep shock. Towards the end of the week, Darnley was buried in James V's vault in Holyrood Abbey. He was only 21. Meanwhile, such was Mary's state of nervous collapse that her doctors insisted that she leave her mourning room and go and stay at Seton, further along the Forth estuary, to try to improve her health. They no doubt remembered how her father had suffered a similar collapse and had died soon after the shock of his army being defeated at Solway Moss.

When the English ambassador Henry Killigrew had an audience with Mary a month after the explosion, he reported that her voice and her manner still showed signs of profound grief. However, the rumours had begun only a week after the assassination. Placards began to appear throughout the town, accusing Bothwell of murdering Darnley, and, on 1 March, a new theme emerged. A drawing was pinned up, showing a crowned mermaid and a hare standing in a circle of swords. This means nothing to us now, but people were accustomed to such symbols in the sixteenth century, and they recognised the message right away. The mermaid represented a prostitute, the crown indicated that this prostitute was the queen, and a hare was the animal on Bothwell's family crest. The accusation was that the queen and Bothwell were lovers, and that they had murdered Darnley so that they could marry.

So how had Mary's relationship with Darnley, which had begun so well, ended in tragedy and these devastating charges against her? Ever since the assassination of David Rizzio, the relationship between the queen and her husband had steadily deteriorated. The morning after the Italian's death on 9 March 1566, Darnley had pleaded with Mary to forgive him, declaring that he was young and inexperienced and had been tricked by traitors. Somehow, she must save them both. Bitterly, she had replied that she could never forget what had happened but, six months pregnant as she was, she managed to devise a plan for her escape from the palace and she took him with her, telling him that, as the father of her coming child, she would never abandon him. After a ride of five hours they arrived safely at Dunbar. By apparently reconciling with him, she divided her enemies and she was able to return to Edinburgh in mid-March.

With the danger to himself seemingly over, Darnley soon returned to his old ways, and there were rumours that Mary would divorce him. He was hated by all the lords now, and he constantly compromised his own security by bathing in secluded coves of the Forth estuary as well as endangering the queen herself by staying out until all hours, so that the gates of Edinburgh Castle, where Mary had moved for greater safety in the aftermath of the Rizzio murder, had to be left open until he returned. According to Mary's own account, she tried to keep an eye on him by being with him as much as she could, and she even agreed to sleep with him again, but there was no affection left between them. In July 1566, they quarrelled publicly during a stag hunt at Traquair, in the Borders, and Darnley began to speak of going to live on his relatives' estates in France. This would have been a dreadful insult to the queen and, when he started a campaign to try to

Stirling, his christening overshadowed by yet another quarrel between his parents, which resulted in Darnley refusing to attend the service.

Darnley then left in the huff, making for his father's part of the country in the west of Scotland. On Christmas Eve, he fell ill in Glasgow. His disease was diagnosed as being smallpox, and Mary sent her doctor to him. It would have been far too dangerous for her to go to him in person, for she might have caught the infection or passed it on to her baby son. Many historians now believe that his illness had a different origin and that he was actually suffering from syphilis. He seems to have been treated with mercury, the standard remedy for secondary syphilis, and this was followed by special medicinal baths. On about 22 January 1567, Mary finally arrived in Glasgow to see him. He was pathetically pleased, and she gave him the impression that she wanted them to reconcile. She would take him back to Edinburgh, where he could stay in the nearby Craigmillar Castle and, when he was completely better, he would join her and their son in Holyroodhouse. They would be husband and wife once more.

The two duly set off for Edinburgh, Darnley lying in a litter drawn by horses, Mary presumably riding. Her plan to take him to Craigmillar Castle had suffered a reverse when he had refused to stay there because he hated its keeper, Sir Simon Preston, and feared that Preston might be plotting against him. However, he now agreed to stay at Kirk o' Field instead. Mary had furnishings sent up from Holyroodhouse for him, and a bath was installed beside his bed for his continuing medical treatment. He was settled there on 1 February and his special baths were to continue for another ten days.

During that time, Mary visited him regularly, and they appeared to be on the best of terms. She went one last time, on the fatal evening of 9 February, and they chatted happily about his return to Holyrood the following day. Then she left to go to the wedding celebrations. The lords, of course, were perfectly well aware of what was intended. Moray made sure that he was out of Edinburgh on the night of 9 February, as did Sir William Maitland of Lethington. Just as Rizzio's murder had been known about in London before it took place, so Queen Elizabeth's ministers knew exactly what was going to happen at Kirk o' Field. Elizabeth herself probably did not. Like Mary, she would have reacted indignantly to any thought of an attack upon a king consort, however inadequate he might be.

Is there, then, any documentary evidence proving that the queen and Bothwell had an affair and that she was indeed guilty of adultery and murder? In 1569, a year after her flight to England, an investigation into the charges against her was held at York. There, the Earl of Moray and his friends would voice their accusations, and Elizabeth and her advisers would decide whether she was guilty or innocent. Elizabeth did not preside over the enquiry in person, and Mary was not allowed to attend, but she was represented by seven commissioners led by John Leslie, Bishop of Ross. The proceedings were moved to Westminster later in the year, and, on 7 December, Moray formally produced an ornate silver casket purporting to contain irrefutable documentary evidence of her guilt.

This was said to have been in the possession of George Dalgleish, one of the Earl of Bothwell's retainers. Inside it were two marriage contracts between Mary and Bothwell, some love sonnets she had allegedly written, and eight apparently incriminating letters from her to him. Unfortunately, these documents disappeared without trace in the 1580s and have never been seen since. We know them only from copies and translations from the original French made during the Westminster enquiry. There is therefore no chance of examining the original handwriting to see if they were genuinely written by Mary. What soon becomes clear, however, is the erratic nature of the texts. These have been studied many times. In the past, some historians believed that they were straightforward forgeries, but now the consensus is that there were sections of genuine letters by Mary mixed in with parts of other letters to Bothwell from one of his discarded mistresses, and possibly some forged additions as well.

Elizabeth I's commissioners were particularly shocked by the longest letter, written from Glasgow to Bothwell and apparently showing that Mary and Bothwell plotted Darnley's death. According to its text, Mary is visiting Darnley with the sole objective of bringing him back to Edinburgh. He is desperate for a reconciliation, and she says that, if she had not known of his treachery, she might have been taken in by his blandishments. As it is, she realises that he is totally unreliable. She hates having to deceive him, because deceit is not in her nature, she says, but she knows what she has to do. In much of this lengthy letter, we seem to be hearing Mary's authentic voice, but there are other unsettling aspects to it. The text is disjointed and there are very obvious inconsistencies. More importantly, however, although the letter expresses extreme distaste for her husband and is obviously written to a close friend, it contains no hint that the queen was luring Darnley back to Edinburgh in order to murder him. In fact, as John Guy her biographer has pointed out, no one has ever found a single piece of uncontaminated evidence proving that Mary knew of Darnley's murder in advance.

So was Mary guilty or innocent of complicity in the murder of Darnley? There are three possible explanations for her behaviour. One is that she was entirely unaware of any plot and brought Darnley back to Edinburgh because she genuinely wanted a reconciliation with him, believing it to be her only option. That is possible, but unlikely. She was completely disillusioned with him, and she certainly would not have intended to sleep with him again if she thought or knew that he really had syphilis. The second possibility is that she was an accessory to murder, and lured Darnley to Kirk o' Field so that Bothwell could kill him. That was what her enemies believed. The third possibility is that she was well aware that Darnley was already plotting against her again, this time planning to have her imprisoned so that he could rule Scotland on behalf of their infant son. She urgently needed to bring him back to Edinburgh, where a watch could be kept on him until such time as a separation from him could be arranged; and she was relying on her lords to accomplish this.

In this connection, it is interesting to note that Lady Lennox was so distraught at the death of her son that she and her husband commissioned a huge painting showing his effigy lying on his tomb, with the figure of little Prince James in the foreground calling for vengeance. However, in her later years, the impossible seems to have happened, and she and Mary were apparently reconciled. Imprisoned in the Tower of London by Elizabeth I for having arranged her younger son's marriage without royal permission, Lady Lennox corresponded with the captive Mary, signing herself 'Your Majesty's most humble and loving mother and aunt'. Arch-plotter that she was, it is nevertheless hard to believe that she could ever have put on a semblance of friendship for Mary had she not become convinced that Mary was innocent of any part in Darnley's death.

Whatever the true explanation, in the weeks after Darnley's murder, Mary became more and more isolated as her supporters and even her family in France distanced themselves from the crime. They warned her that, in order to save her reputation, she must immediately take action and prosecute the Earl of Bothwell, the man now identified as the chief suspect, but she did not do so. Instead, she married him.

Chapter 7

Did the Earl of Bothwell abduct Mary?

FACTS

So what was James, Earl of Bothwell really like? When the other lords saw that Mary, Queen of Scots trusted him and relied on him for advice, they were jealous and put about stories of him being crude and unprincipled. In fact, he was reasonably sophisticated compared with many of his contemporaries. His father had been a loyal supporter of Mary of Guise and had even hoped at one time to marry her. Bothwell's parents were divorced before he was ten years old, and he was then sent to Spynie Castle in Moray to be brought up by his great-uncle, the energetic and irascible Patrick Hepburn, Bishop of Moray, father of at least thirteen illegitimate children by a variety of partners. When the boy reached his teens, the bishop announced that he should complete his education on the continent and dispatched him to Paris, where he studied military history, became fluent in French and adopted the sort of elegant, italic style of handwriting favoured by the French aristocracy.

At the age of 21, he succeeded his father as Earl of Bothwell, hereditary Lord High Admiral of Scotland and hereditary sheriff of Berwick and Haddington as well as of Edinburgh. Two years after that, he was made Lieutenant of the Border with England. He was a public figure from an early age and it soon became obvious that he was both ambitious and reckless. We have no full-length portrait of him, but in the Scottish National Portrait Gallery there is a tiny miniature of him, about the size of a 50p piece, painted in oil on copper. It shows a tough-looking character with a wary expression and a broken nose. He was certainly not handsome, and contemporaries described him as being ape-like in appearance, but although he was short he was very muscular, full of energy and apparently irresistible to women. He was only 24 when he had an affair with 43-year-old Janet Beaton, who had been married three times, had seven children and was rather alarmingly known as 'the Wizard Lady of Branxholm'.

Despite the fact that he was a Protestant, Bothwell was an energetic supporter of Mary of Guise. In fact, in 1559 he even managed to intercept £3,000 being sent by Elizabeth I of England to the Scottish Protestant lords, and gave the money to Mary of Guise instead. He helped to defend Leith against the English the following year, and then he was sent to France to try to obtain further military assistance for the queen regent. After her death he did not hurry home but lingered in Copenhagen, where he had an affair with Anna Throndsen, daughter of a retired admiral. She was desperately in love with him, and he promised to marry her. Together they travelled to Paris, and there he met Mary, Queen of Scots, who was at that time still married to François II of France. No doubt, when he spoke to her, he made the most of his past helpfulness to her mother and he was given 600 gold coins and made a gentleman of François's bedchamber. He seems to have spent the next few months in Flanders with Anna but, when François died and Mary, Queen of Scots decided to return to Scotland, he escorted her on her voyage in his official capacity as Lord High Admiral.

Nicholas Throckmorton, the English ambassador in Paris, had already warned Elizabeth I that Bothwell was a rash and dangerous young man whose enemies should keep an eye on him, but Mary valued his loyalty. Home again in Scotland, she made him a member of her Privy Council, although when he became involved in a fracas with the young, mentally unstable Earl of Arran she had him arrested and thrown into prison. Somehow, he managed to escape from Edinburgh Castle and set sail aboard a merchant ship for France, only to be captured at sea by the English and put in the Tower of London. Mary and the French managed to have him released, and she recommended him for the vacant post of captain of the Royal Guard of Scottish Archers, who formed part of the French king's bodyguard. During a brief return to Scotland, he soon found himself in trouble again and fled to France once more, but Mary needed him to support her planned marriage to Lord Darnley and recalled him.

Bothwell accompanied the royal couple on the 'Chaseabout Raid', when they drove the rebellious Earl of Moray out of Scotland. By this time, Bothwell was deeply in debt, but the following year the queen found a way of solving his financial difficulties. She arranged for him to marry Lady Jean Gordon, sister of his great friend the 5th Earl of Huntly. Jean was in love with someone else, but arranged marriages were the norm, and the contract noted that it was drawn up with the express advice of Mary, Queen of Scots. She was the first to sign the document, and the wedding took place on 24 February 1566. The bride was a member of a leading Catholic family, and the queen had particularly requested a Catholic ceremony, but Bothwell insisted on a Protestant service. He then used almost all his bride's large dowry to reclaim his lands of Crichton, which he had been forced to give in pledge to his creditors.

At first, Bothwell's married life seemed to be unremarkable, but, as far as he was concerned, his wife had served her purpose, and his thoughts were elsewhere. He knew all about the difficulties in the queen's marriage, and he already saw himself as Darnley's successor. He encouraged Mary to regard him as her strong protector but, while it is true that, in a world of shifting loyalties, he never did desert her cause, she was first and foremost his means of furthering his own ambitions. As for Mary herself, his unwavering support came as a great relief to her in an environment where she had found that she could trust no one. She later described him as a man of resolution who was well adapted to rule, but it is highly unlikely that she saw him as a possible husband at that stage. He was not of royal descent and she still had no intention of marrying a mere subject, but did the two become lovers?

After the murder of Darnley on 10 February 1567, the same sort of gossip which had linked her name with Rizzio's now swirled around Mary and Bothwell. When she was told about the placards accusing Bothwell of the Darnley murder, she was highly indignant that her loyal friend was being slandered by the very men whom she believed to be guilty of the crime, and she quickly defended him. Convinced that her enemies had meant that she too should die that night at Kirk o' Field and that her life was in imminent danger, she needed this strong protector more than ever. Such was her trust in him that, when she moved to Seton for the sake of her health, she left her baby son in the care of Bothwell and his brother-in-law Huntly. She continued to consult him about affairs of state, gave him presents and declined to prosecute him for Darnley's murder, leaving it instead to the dead man's father, the Earl of Lennox, to accuse him.

Bothwell's trial took place on 12 April 1567 in Edinburgh Tolbooth. Lennox was not present, because he had been told that he could not enter the capital with more than half a dozen companions. He knew that Edinburgh was packed with Bothwell's supporters and, eager as he was for vengeance, he would have risked being assassinated himself if he had appeared. The proceedings therefore took place in the absence of both Lennox, who remained in the west of Scotland, and the queen, who stayed in Holyroodhouse.

The trial lasted for more than eight hours, and in the end Bothwell was acquitted. Four days later, when Mary opened parliament, he walked in her procession carrying the sceptre.

Bothwell was convinced that there was now no obstacle in the way of his great ambition. In the weeks that followed, he is said to have proposed to the queen on several occasions, although still married to his wife. Each time, Mary refused him. Not to be diverted, he gathered a group of leading men, probably in Ainslie's Tavern in Edinburgh, and forced them to sign an agreement declaring that he was innocent of any part in Darnley's murder and advising the queen to marry him. Eight bishops, ten earls and eleven lords signed this new bond, protesting afterwards that their signatures had been extorted from them because the building had been surrounded by Bothwell's armed followers. Even then, Mary hesitated. Although she still did not believe that he was Darnley's murderer, she knew that his reputation was tainted. However, the thought of a strong, masculine consort who would safeguard her and her son against her treacherous nobility was irresistible, and she persuaded herself that a marriage to Protestant Bothwell might help to settle the religious divisions within the country. Deserted by her Roman Catholic allies, she had taken the Reformed Church under her protection at the recent parliament.

Even so, Mary seems to have felt that she could not be seen to enter into this marriage of her own free will. Bothwell is often assumed to have planned what followed, but we know that Mary at this point had long talks with

Sir William Maitland of Lethington, that subtle politician known as 'Scotland's Machiavelli'. There is no reliable evidence, but it is possible that the events set in motion on 20 April were of their devising, with Bothwell as a slightly reluctant accomplice. He would probably have seen no reason for a time-consuming deception. His wife had no affection for him and, in the event, he was confident that she would divorce him right away. In fact, each swiftly divorced the other.

Whoever thought up the plan, Mary went to visit Prince James in Stirling Castle, where he was now staying in the care of the Earl of Mar. After spending two or three days there, she set off for Edinburgh with a retinue of about thirty people, including the Earl of Huntly, Maitland of Lethington and Sir James Melville. They were about six miles from Edinburgh when they were intercepted by Bothwell at the head of a small army. He rode up to the queen, grabbed the bridle of her horse and told her that, because there was danger in the capital, he was taking her to the safety of Dunbar Castle. Some of her companions objected but she told them to be quiet. She could bear no more bloodshed, she said. Huntly, Maitland and Melville were taken with her to Dunbar where, according to Melville's account, Bothwell raped her. She herself remarked afterwards that, although she had found his behaviour rude, his words were gentle. Of course, if a staged abduction had been her idea, she would not have intended him to force himself on her, but Bothwell, ever the man of action, no doubt seized his opportunity.

On 6 May 1567, Mary and Bothwell rode into Edinburgh together, he again leading her horse by the bridle as if she

was his prisoner. When one of the Edinburgh ministers
was asked that day to proclaim the banns for her Protestant
marriage to Bothwell, he refused, saying that he believed
that she was being forced into the match against her will.
However, the very next day, the Lord Justice Clerk brought
him a document signed by the queen, saying that she had
neither been kept prisoner nor been raped. She made
Bothwell Duke of Orkney that same week, the marriage
contract was signed on 14 May, and the wedding took
place the next day in the Great Hall of Holyroodhouse. It
was conducted by Bothwell's Protestant friend, the Bishop
of Orkney.

The queen was dressed in deepest mourning for Lord
Darnley, who had been dead for just over three months, and
the wedding meal afterwards took place in an atmosphere
of undiluted gloom. This was no joyous culmination of a
love affair and that afternoon, when Mary met the Roman
Catholic Bishop Leslie, she wept, promising him that she
would never abandon the Catholic Church and saying that
she already regretted having had a Protestant ceremony.
During the days that followed, the queen seemed sombre and
depressed, well aware that she had ruined her reputation.
Her own Dominican confessor swore that summer to the
Spanish ambassador in London that, until the question of
her marriage with Bothwell was raised, he had never seen
a woman of greater virtue, courage and uprightness. The
choice of Bothwell as her third husband was disastrous. Her
remaining friends deserted her, people everywhere took it
as proof that she was guilty of adultery with him and of the
murder of Darnley, and the lords who had encouraged the

marriage were now consumed with jealousy of him. They never stopped criticising his allegedly boorish behaviour towards her, and they began to demand that she put him away.

Both sides raised armies, and the two forces confronted each other at Carberry Hill on 15 June, exactly a month after the wedding. Above the lords' army fluttered a huge white banner with a picture of Darnley's body lying beneath the tree, and little Prince James kneeling nearby, calling for vengeance. In the end, Mary's army began to drift off and she surrendered to her lords, sending Bothwell away and telling him that he must not come back until parliament had investigated the murder of Darnley and proved him innocent or guilty. If the former, nothing would prevent her from living as his lawful wife, she said, but if the latter, it would be an endless source of regret to her that, by marrying him, she had ruined her reputation. She would try to free herself by every possible means.

Bothwell rode north, hoping to gather ships to come to the queen's assistance but, pursued as a traitor, he was forced to flee to Scandinavia. His subsequent attempts to enlist the support of Frederick II of Denmark came to nothing, and he spent the rest of his life as a prisoner there. Meanwhile, Mary was imprisoned in Lochleven Castle and forced to abdicate. The following year she escaped, only to be defeated by her Protestant lords at the Battle of Langside. Fleeing from the field, she insisted on making her way to England, confident that Elizabeth I would help her and provide her with an army to restore her to her throne. Instead, she found that she was a captive.

So did the Casket Letters have anything to offer about Bothwell's alleged seizure of the queen and the subsequent rape? Three short messages, apparently written by Mary from Stirling before the abduction, are so full of inconsistencies and unconvincing statements that they cannot be taken as evidence. The eighth Casket Letter seems to show her worrying about whether her own retinue might prevent her from being taken away, and urging Bothwell to make sure that he had enough followers with him. No complete copy of the original French version survives, and as usual there are inconsistencies and discrepancies. All four letters seem to show Bothwell being indecisive and slow to act, which was entirely uncharacteristic, unless the plot had indeed been thought up by Maitland and Mary and he was doubtful about it. Also, it must be significant that Mary's accusers did not use the three short letters against her, and indeed they even told the English ambassador that she had been forced to become the bedfellow of another woman's husband.

In recent years, the arguments about the abduction have focused on an additional reason why Mary might have been willing to collude in the abduction plot. When Lord Lindsay and Lord Ruthven forced her to sign her abdication document, she was lying in bed in Lochleven Castle, almost too weak to move, after a serious haemorrhage caused by miscarrying twins, the children of Bothwell. This detail comes from the reminiscences she dictated to her secretary, Claude Nau, many years later during her English imprisonment. A medical historian in the early twentieth century suggested that the babies must have been conceived while Darnley was still alive, and this idea was taken up with alacrity by various historians because it would have proved Mary's adultery with Bothwell. However, it has subsequently been pointed out that, if the miscarriage had occurred about five months, then it would have been quite impossible for the queen to conceal her condition throughout the spring. Female monarchs were constantly scrutinised by servants and courtiers to see if they were pregnant, and there was no way that Mary could have hidden her increasing size for such a long time.

Mary claimed that the twins were conceived immediately after her marriage because she was desperate that they should not be seen as illegitimate, thereby destroying her reputation. However, that date of conception is unlikely too. Sir John Dewhurst, Professor of Obstetrics and Gynaecology at London University, explained that twin foetuses of eight or nine weeks' gestation would be most unlikely to be recognised, and even more so when there was heavy bleeding. He therefore agreed with Lady Antonia Fraser's conclusion that the twins must have been conceived when or immediately after Bothwell forced himself on Mary at Dunbar. Foetuses grow rapidly in the early months of pregnancy, and at twelve weeks they would have been twice as big as when they were only nine weeks old. Although there can be no certainty about the date of conception, it does appear that we can dismiss the speculation that Mary needed to marry Bothwell at the time of Darnley's murder because she was already pregnant. Had there been anything as suspicious as that, she would never have mentioned the miscarriage at all in the memoirs she dictated to Nau, which are in fact the only source of information about the twins.

We are left, of course, with the question of whether Mary really had fallen in love with Bothwell. It is perfectly possible that she did, for she was a woman of passionate emotions. The real question is to what extent she would have thrown away all other considerations in order to be with him. Her critics think that she was so infatuated that she became Bothwell's mistress during Darnley's lifetime. Her defenders believe that this did not happen and that she only agreed to marry him because her life had fallen apart: her consort had been murdered, and she and her baby son were in danger of being kidnapped if not assassinated. She desperately needed a reliable protector. Her behaviour after her wedding to Bothwell hardly suggests a triumphant accomplice in murder achieving her greatest desire. It must also be relevant that, as a captive in England in October 1568, only seventeen months after she and Bothwell married, she was willing to divorce him in the hope that Elizabeth I would then help to restore her to her Scottish throne. We shall probably never know how she really felt, but then the mysteries are exactly what lend such fascination to the story of Mary, Queen of Scots.

Chapter 8

Did Mary and Queen Elizabeth I of England ever meet?

MYTH

When Mary, Queen of Scots fled to England after her defeat at the Battle of Langside in 1568, she expected Elizabeth I to help her, but instead she was held prisoner. During her captivity, she and Elizabeth had a secret meeting, but Mary failed to convince the English queen that she was innocent of the Darnley murder, and she remained a prisoner until Elizabeth had her executed in 1587.

FACTS

Throughout her adult life, Mary, Queen of Scots believed that, because they were fellow monarchs, she and Elizabeth I could overlook their differences. As Mary put it to the English ambassador before she left France in 1561, she and his queen would be living in the same island, both speaking the same language and each was the nearest female relative that the other had. This was not strictly true, of course, since Mary spoke Scots rather than English and thought in French; nor did either of them entirely lack female relatives.

There was Lady Lennox, for instance, who was Elizabeth's first cousin and Mary's aunt, not to mention Mary's half-sister the Countess of Argyll. However, these were minor considerations compared with what really mattered: the English succession.

It has often been said that Mary was naïve in seeking Elizabeth's friendship, but in fact it was a carefully considered policy, and Mary's attitude to the English queen was from the start mingled with a certain derision and dislike. As we have seen, there was, for instance, the occasion in 1561 when Elizabeth refused to grant Mary the safe conduct to sail back to Scotland. Mary had heard all about Elizabeth's angry reaction to the request and, when Sir Nicholas Throckmorton, the English ambassador, next came to see her in Paris, she told him loudly in front of a crowd of courtiers that he and she must move away from the others before he spoke. It would never do, she remarked sweetly, if he said something to annoy her and she gave an exhibition of petulance and bad temper. Everyone knew exactly who had done that.

Elizabeth, of course, saw their situation very differently. The fact that the two were fellow monarchs struck a deep chord with her, but she was going to be all the more difficult to win over because she had been insecure from childhood. She very well knew that, as Anne Boleyn's daughter, she was considered by Roman Catholics to be illegitimate, with no right to the English throne. She had therefore been highly alarmed and enraged when Henri II of France started putting Mary, Queen of Scots forward as the rightful queen of England. Always wary, she would find it very difficult to trust

Mary, but various historians, including Lady Antonia Fraser and John Guy, have argued persuasively that Elizabeth was much more sympathetic to Mary than has previously been recognised. The position of monarch is always a lonely one, and it was particularly difficult in the sixteenth century for a woman. The thought of a friendship with someone who was in the same position must have been as tempting to Elizabeth as it was to Mary, but her strongly Protestant advisers, led by Sir William Cecil, were absolutely determined that no concession should ever be offered to the Catholic Queen of Scots.

As we have seen in Chapter 2, there can be little doubt that the succession to the English throne was at the forefront of Mary's mind even before she returned to her native land. However, she seems to have been genuinely content to play a waiting game. She knew perfectly well that she was in no position to challenge Elizabeth for her throne. Even with French help, she would never be able to muster an army to march into England and depose the English queen. Ruling her own divided country was going to be enough of a challenge. There were also other factors to consider, one of them being the age gap between the two women. Elizabeth had been the cousin of Mary's father.

There were just nine years between Elizabeth and Mary, it was true, but although Elizabeth was still only in her late twenties when Mary returned from France to begin her personal rule, that was considered to be a much more mature age in the sixteenth century than it is now. Many women would have been married for twelve or thirteen years by then, and this was all the more significant for a queen who must produce heirs to her throne. There were already rumours that Elizabeth did not want to share her power with any husband and was in any case physically incapable of having children. Mary therefore decided, reasonably enough, that her best hope of being nominated as Elizabeth's successor was to make friends with her.

With the benefit of hindsight, we might think that this was an unrealistic ambition, but Mary had good enough reason to hope for success. Throughout her life, she had been praised and admired for her attractiveness and her charm. She had her father's gift of being able to talk to people from all ranks of society, and, if she had not pleased everyone, she had confidence in her ability to win over even the initially hostile. Now, she was prepared to go to great lengths to befriend her difficult rival. Her tone in her letters to Elizabeth at that time was always polite and respectful, and she was adept at finding ways to please. While she was still the wife of François II, she was eager to exchange portraits with Elizabeth and, when the English ambassador arrived to offer condolences after the death of François and urged her to ratify the Treaty of Edinburgh, Mary replied that she was anxious to meet her fellow queen in person. If they could discuss their differences face to face, without the need for male intermediaries, they could reach an agreement much more quickly, she felt sure.

Mary returned to this theme once she was back in Scotland, possibly encouraged by the fact that one of her principal advisers, William Maitland of Lethington, was an enthusiastic supporter of an alliance with England. He dreamed of a union of the two countries which would put an end to the centuries of warfare between them and, a mere two weeks after Mary's return, he was sent to London to say that the Queen of Scots would ratify the Treaty of Edinburgh recognising Elizabeth as queen of England, provided that she in her turn recognised Mary as her heir. This did not elicit the agreement that Mary hoped for, and in January 1562 she repeated the offer, once again suggesting that she and Elizabeth should meet in person to discuss the matter. Both the Scottish and the English statesmen had their doubts about the plan. There was no knowing what might happen if those two royal women got together. Cecil was afraid that Elizabeth would succumb to Mary's famous charm and be won over to her point of view, while Maitland feared that Mary would be outmanoeuvred because she was so much younger and less experienced than Elizabeth.

That did not stop Mary. She continued her campaign, exchanging rings with Elizabeth and sending flattering letters and at least one poem which she probably composed herself. Although Elizabeth was characteristically suspicious at first, she became surprisingly enthusiastic, and arrangements were made for the historic encounter to take place in Nottingham on 3 September 1562. By July, however, Elizabeth had changed her mind. Mary's uncle, the Duke of Guise, was persecuting French Protestants and so, she said, she could not possibly enter into negotiations with that man's niece. Some historians suspect that this was merely an excuse. Cecil and his colleagues had been very worried by the thought of Mary coming with a huge retinue to the north of England, where there was a good deal of Catholic support. There was also the possibility that Elizabeth did not want unflattering comparisons to be made between herself and her younger and more glamorous rival. Whatever the reason, the plans for Nottingham were cancelled, leaving Mary bitterly disappointed. However, when Elizabeth then sent word that the meeting could be rescheduled for the following summer in Nottingham or in York or some other place suggested by the Queen of Scots, her hopes rose again.

A few weeks later, in October 1562, Elizabeth fell seriously ill. She had contracted smallpox, and there was panic in the English court. Suddenly, everyone was having to think about the succession to the throne, and the comments of the Spanish ambassador in London on this subject are particularly interesting. He was of the opinion that, should Elizabeth die, there was no obvious heir to succeed her. Some Catholics favoured Mary, Queen of Scots, he reported but, given England's long history of hostility to France, others preferred the Countess of Lennox while, of course, the Protestants wanted neither. Elizabeth recovered, but Mary must have seen that she would have to redouble her efforts if the rival candidates were to be dismissed.

The relationship between the two queens became even more difficult when the question of Mary's remarriage arose, for Elizabeth would have liked to dictate the choice of husband, and her personal jealousy of Mary was a complicating factor. When Elizabeth saw Sir James Melville at the time when she was suggesting Darnley as an appropriate suitor for Mary, she took the opportunity of quizzing him about his queen's appearance. What did she look like? What colour was her hair? Elizabeth's was red-gold, but Mary's was only auburn. Which of them was the fairer? Sir James replied carefully that Elizabeth was the fairest in England and Mary was the fairest in Scotland. Which was the taller? Mary was the taller, he said. Then she was too tall, replied Elizabeth smugly, she herself being neither too tall nor too short. When he mentioned that Mary was musical and played on both the lute and the virginals, Elizabeth so arranged things that, whenever he accidentally came upon her, she was dancing, playing an instrument or engaged in some other display of her talents.

In the end, Mary married Lord Darnley. When their son was born, she sent Sir James Melville to London to tell Elizabeth. He found her dancing energetically with her courtiers, so he gave the news to Sir William Cecil, who went over to her and whispered it to her. She immediately sank on to a chair, rested her cheek on her hand and for a long time said nothing. At last, she remarked in melancholy tones that the Queen of Scots was lighter of a fair son whereas she herself was barren. However, she knew the dynastic significance of this child who had both royal Tudor and royal Stewart blood in his veins, and she agreed to be one of his godparents, along with the king of France and the Duke of Savoy. She would not attend the christening herself but, despite a reputation for meanness, she sent a very lavish gift, a huge gold and enamelled font set with precious stones.

After that, Mary's personal rule in Scotland quickly un-ravelled. On the afternoon of Sunday 16 May 1568, following her defeat at the Battle of Langside, she and a small group of supporters led by Lord Herries went down from Dundrennan Abbey to the shores of the Solway estuary and boarded a fishing boat. They arrived in England four hours later and spent the night in Workington Hall, which belonged to a friend of Lord Herries. Next morning, the Deputy Governor of Carlisle arrived with a detachment of several hundred horsemen and escorted the queen to Carlisle Castle. Mary was alarmed. She was intent on going straight to London to beg Elizabeth I for help, but, instead of the friendly welcome she expected, she found that she was held prisoner in rooms with gratings on the windows and soldiers guarding the doors. On 8 June, a messenger arrived from London to tell her that Elizabeth could not receive her.

These events lent a desperate urgency to Mary's desire to meet Elizabeth in person. In reply to her increasingly distraught messages, she was told that an enquiry into her alleged crimes would be held in York. She received this news with happy confidence. Of course she would be totally exonerated, and then she would be free to go and see Elizabeth. Her optimism abruptly vanished, however, when she heard that the Earl of Moray, her own half-brother, was to be her chief accuser, and that he was bringing to York with him the mysterious casket containing letters which would incriminate her. She never was allowed to see the letters. In the end, the enquiry, by that time moved to Westminster, could reach no conclusion. The final report said that Mary had failed to prove that her subjects had unjustly rebelled against her, but Moray had likewise failed to prove that she had been implicated in Darnley's death. The difference was that Moray was then free to return to Scotland, while Mary remained a prisoner.

Throughout the long and tedious years of her captivity, the Queen of Scots wrote many letters to the Queen of

England. The letters were long, they were eloquent and at first they were hopeful. They pleaded for a meeting, they protested Mary's innocence of any crime and they stressed her sincerity. She needed help to regain her throne, her poor supporters in Scotland were being persecuted and surely, as her cousin and fellow queen, Elizabeth would help her. Sometimes little gifts accompanied the letters, and once there was even a poem Mary had written in French, describing her plight. Some historians believe that, in the early days, Elizabeth probably did mean to restore Mary to the Scottish throne, but as the years went by, all hope of that ebbed away when one plot after another was discovered, the aim of all of them being to depose Elizabeth and place Mary on the English throne instead.

Her health much impaired by being confined in a series of damp, uncomfortable castles, in 1573 Mary gained permission to visit the baths at Buxton in Derbyshire, famous since Roman times for treating rheumatism and similar conditions. Not only were the medicinal qualities of the water to be valued. London courtiers regularly sought their benefit, and in 1575 Mary even met William Cecil there and the royal favourite, Robert Dudley, Earl of Leicester. Tantalisingly, we have no record of what took place between them, but Cecil seems to have been suspected of becoming friendly with the Scottish queen. Mary undoubtedly lived in hope that Elizabeth herself might visit the town, but the nearest the two queens ever came to each other was when, in 1575, Elizabeth's summer progress took her to Stafford and the manor house of Chartley, not far from the part of the country where Mary was held.

The two queens never did meet, so why is there the persistent story that they did? That particular myth is the result of Friedrich Schiller's famous play, *Maria Stuart*, first performed in Weimar, where he lived, in 1800. Schiller was Professor of History at the University of Jena as well as being a celebrated dramatist with a particular interest in faith and in the psychology of people experiencing crisis. These themes were central to *Maria Stuart,* which has as its powerful climax a scene in which Mary and Elizabeth finally meet. This imaginary encounter is no sentimental piece of fiction but a strong, dramatic sequence weaving into the speeches the crucial features of their relationship: the succession to the English throne, the religious conflict, the fraught events of Mary's past life and her doomed attempts at friendliness with Elizabeth.

It is very cleverly done. The scene is set near Fotheringhay Castle. Mary, already sentenced to death, is one day allowed outside and revels in the fresh air. She hears the noise of a hunt approaching, and suddenly she is told that Elizabeth has come to see her in response to her latest letter. The shock is almost too much for her, for she has for so long hoped for such an opportunity and been so many times disappointed. However, she gathers her strength and, when Elizabeth appears, kneels at her feet and begs for her freedom. In a lengthy speech, she describes how she has been unjustly held captive and protests that it is the fault of neither of them, but of fate.

At first, Elizabeth is very much in control of the interview, but, when she begins to blame not fate but Mary's Roman Catholic relatives and her past behaviour, the Queen of Scots suddenly takes the initiative, indignantly declaring that her own faults were the faults of youth and inexperience. No longer a humble petitioner for her life, she speaks with majestic ferocity, insulting Elizabeth's mother Anne Boleyn and finally declaring that Elizabeth has stolen the throne of England. It is she, Mary, who is Elizabeth's queen, not the other way round. Defeated, Elizabeth flees from the scene while Mary is left as the moral victor of the encounter, at the same time realising that she has made her own execution inevitable.

In the twenty-first century, Schiller's play is still being performed with great success, as in the 2005 London version with Janet McTeer as Mary and Harriet Walter as Elizabeth, and then the following year in the National Theatre of Scotland production with Siobhan Redmond and Catherine Cusack in those roles. The story has also gained even wider fame through Donizetti's 1834 opera, *Maria Stuarda*, which is based on Schiller's text. It is hardly surprising that the myth of the meeting between the two queens has persisted to this day. Misleading as it undoubtedly is, it reminds us that myths can be enlightening, and Schiller's exploration of the central issues not merely seizes the attention but indicates that there is such a thing as artistic truth as well as factual accuracy.

Chapter 9

Did James VI hate his mother, Mary, Queen of Scots?

MYTH

Before he was a year old, the boy's mother and her lover murdered his father, and he never saw her again. Instead, he was brought up by his tutors to hate her. That was the childhood of James VI. He never had anything to do with Mary, Queen of Scots and he was not in the least upset when she was executed, because all he cared about was inheriting the throne of England from Elizabeth I.

FACTS

In the spring of 1566, Mary, Queen of Scots was staying in Edinburgh Castle, her formidable fortress, for greater security. Her baby was due very soon, and on 3 June she took to her bedchamber to await the birth. Her midwife, Margaret Asteane, was with her, and Mary sent to Dunfermline Abbey for the relics of a previous queen, St Margaret, which she hoped would help her in her labour. Childbirth was a dangerous business in the sixteenth century and she took the precaution of making her will as she waited. If she died but the baby survived, everything was to go to the child but, if the baby died too, then her most splendid jewels would become the property of the crown, for future generations of monarchs. She also made dozens of smaller bequests to relatives and friends.

Just over a fortnight later, on 18 June, her contractions started. She would give birth not in her bedchamber, where she would later recover, but in a tiny chamber which can still be seen to this day. A portrait of James VI hangs on the wall, with the year of his birth painted above it. There is no space in that little room for anything more than a bed. Mary's labour continued throughout the night and, when the relics of St Margaret seemed to be doing no good, one of her ladies, the Countess of Atholl, helpfully tried some black magic and attempted to transfer the queen's pains to Lady Reres instead. That did not work either but, between ten and eleven the next morning, the baby was born safely, a fine healthy son.

As soon as Sir James Melville had set off for London to tell Queen Elizabeth I, the birth was announced publicly, the guns in the castle fired a salute and bonfires were lit right across Scotland. Exhausted but triumphant, the queen lost no time in summoning Lord Darnley. It was then that she assured him before the assembled company that this baby was his and no other man's. She also turned to Sir William Stanley, an Englishman who was present, telling him that she hoped this son of hers would one day be the first to unite the kingdoms of Scotland and England.

Proud as she was of her child, there was no question of Mary looking after him herself. As was usual with royal babies, he had a wet-nurse to suckle him from the day of his birth. He thrived, and on 17 December 1566, when he was six months old, he was baptised by John Hamilton, Archbishop of St Andrews, in a Roman Catholic ceremony in the Chapel Royal at Stirling Castle. He was given the names Charles James – Charles for Charles IX, king of France, who was one of his godfathers, and James, the traditional name for a King of Scots. George Buchanan, the neo-classical poet,composed a Latin masque to entertain the large gathering at the banquet afterwards. Perhaps it was a sign of Mary's affection for her son that she took him with her to Holyroodhouse after Christmas while Darnley lay ill in Glasgow.

On 9 March 1567, when the prince was nine months old and a month after his father's murder, Mary gave him into the care of John, 1st Earl of Mar, to be brought up in Stirling Castle. This was the customary practice for the heir to the throne. It would be far too dangerous for monarch and heir to live in the same place permanently, because then they might perish together in any assassination attempt. Mar was a Protestant, but Mary knew and liked him. Indeed, it was she who had given him his earldom that day in 1565 when she married Lord Darnley. Her precious child would be safe in his care and indeed, although Mar's loyalty to Mary ended when she married Bothwell, he remained faithful to his task of guarding her son. When James had been in Stirling for six weeks or so, Mary rode there to visit him. It was when she was on her way back to Edinburgh that she was allegedly carried off by Bothwell, and she and her son never saw each other again.

On 29 July 1567, five days after Mary's enforced abdication at Lochleven, Prince James was crowned King of Scots. The ceremony took place in the Church of the Holy Rude in Stirling, and for the first time ever in Scotland it was a Protestant coronation, with John Knox preaching the sermon. The Earl of Morton took an oath on the little king's behalf, promising that James would uphold the Reformed faith. Mary protested vehemently when she heard the news. Her child could not be king as long as she was alive. She had signed her abdication, it was true, but it had been extracted from her by force and, as the English ambassador, Sir Nicholas Throckmorton, had told her, any documents to which she put her signature in those circumstances would have no validity.

Mary's half-brother, the Earl of Moray, now became regent of Scotland and, as a leading Protestant, he made sure that James had a Protestant upbringing. As soon as he was old enough, two tutors were appointed for the boy. The principal one was none other than George Buchanan, who had at one time read the classics with Mary each day and had composed poetry in her honour. Since then, coming from one of the estates owned by Darnley's father, the Earl of Lennox, he had become her bitter enemy and one of her principal accusers. He would now give her little son an astonishingly rigorous education. James had to study Greek before breakfast, Latin afterwards and logic, rhetoric, arithmetic or cosmography in the afternoon.

A highly intelligent child, the king was fluent in French, and by the time he was eight he could easily translate a whole chapter of the Bible from Latin into French and then into

English whenever he was asked. He shared his schoolroom with three other boys, Mar's son John, John's cousin William Murray and another boy named Walter Stewart. Buchanan had no qualms about whipping the young king or boxing his ears if he misbehaved. Long years afterwards, James admitted that he could not help trembling when he saw coming towards him an elderly courtier who reminded him of Buchanan.

Buchanan saw it as his duty to teach James that his adulterous mother had murdered his innocent father. Although Mary, Queen of Scots constantly sent her son letters and presents, the boy was never allowed to see them and they were returned to her, unopened. However, Annabella Murray, the Earl of Mar's wife, had been one of Mary's favourite ladies-in-waiting, and throughout James's childhood she acted as a surrogate mother to the king, protecting him when she could from Buchanan's rages. If she also gave James a kinder image of his absent mother, then this was reinforced by the arrival in Scotland of someone who was to become his admired companion. Esmé Stuart, Seigneur d'Aubigny, first cousin of Lord Darnley, was a member of that branch of the Lennox family which had settled in France. Significantly, he was also a close friend of the Guises. In September 1579, he had received a message, apparently from James VI, inviting him to visit Scotland. The Duke of Guise led the party of French courtiers who saw him off at Dieppe. A few days later, he landed at Leith and was taken to Holyroodhouse to meet the king.

James was 13 years old. Aubigny was about 37, a married man with five young children. Gentle, charming and sophisticated, he delighted the lonely teenager with his kindly concern, treating him as an adult and discussing poetry, theology and politics with him. Whatever he had thought about Lord Darnley, Aubigny was sympathetic to Mary, Queen of Scots, and he would have spoken to James about her and told him from personal knowledge about his Guise relatives. Delighted to discover such an understanding relation, the King gave him the best set of rooms in Holyroodhouse, next to his own. James's grandfather, the Earl of Lennox, was dead by now, and in 1580 the king granted Aubigny the earldom of Lennox and made him chamberlain and first gentleman of the royal chamber. Inevitably, the more popular Lennox became, the more jealous were the Scottish nobles and soon there were all sorts of rumours circulating about the king's new friend. He was a spy of the Duke of Guise, it was said, he meant to make Scotland Roman Catholic again, and he was plotting to restore Mary, Queen of Scots. It was even hinted that he had lured James into a homosexual relationship with him.

Whatever the truth of these stories, Lennox encouraged James to correspond with Mary, Queen of Scots. After years of having her letters returned to her unanswered, she suddenly began to receive messages from him assuring her that this had not been his fault, urging her to give him her advice and promising her that he was her faithful and loyal son. She was overjoyed. At the same time, James did his best to silence the rumours about Lennox, who now converted to Protestantism. In the end, however, Lennox's enemies triumphed, he was forced to leave Scotland in 1582, and he died not long after returning to France. On hearing the news, James was deeply distressed, and composed a long poem mourning his loss. By this time, however, he must have gained a rather different picture of his mother, and he had been alerted to the fact that his Guise relatives were taking a close interest in what was happening to both Mary, Queen of Scots and himself. Indeed, the Duke of Guise was now actively supporting a new plan devised by Mary, whereby she would be restored to the Scottish throne to rule jointly with her son.

This scheme, known as the Association, grew in part from Mary's notion that James was her affectionate and dutiful child who would be delighted to do anything she suggested. She knew that Elizabeth I was eager for a formal alliance with the Scots, and she believed that, during negotiations, James could refuse to have anything to do with an Anglo–Scottish treaty unless his mother was given her freedom. Unfortunately, Mary had an idealised notion of his attitude towards her. When one of his Guise contacts put her suggestion to him, he was at first willing to consider the plan, but that soon changed. He had, after all, been brought up from the age of 13 months to believe that he was the sole King of Scots and no doubt his advisers would have been quick to remind him that Mary remained convinced that her forced abdication was null and void. He was only 15, but he was precocious, and he would have foreseen the many difficulties that her return to Scotland would have created.

Patrick, Master of Gray was employed in the negotiations with Elizabeth. Mary thought that he was reliable, because he had formerly been a member of the household of her ambassador to France, James Beaton, Archbishop of Glasgow, and Gray too was now a close friend of the Guise family. In fact, he proved to be a double agent, and, instead of negotiating with the English on the joint behalf of James and Mary, he abandoned her interests altogether. The following year, James signed a treaty of alliance with England. Far from agreeing to his mother's release, it made no mention of Mary at all, and, to add insult to injury, James even accepted a pension from Elizabeth I. When the news reached her, Mary was appalled. At first, she tried to blame the Master of Gray for betraying her, but she soon came to realise that the fault lay with her son. Raging at his ingratitude, she threatened to disinherit him. The interminable plots by her supporters now seemed to be her only hope of regaining her freedom and, just a fortnight later, she wrote to a young man named Sir Anthony Babington, giving her approval to a plan he was suggesting.

Babington and his friends were Catholic idealists who were dreaming of a foreign invasion which would rescue Mary. What they did not know was that, by this time, her every move was being watched by the agents of Elizabeth's spymaster, Sir Francis Walsingham. The spies swiftly infiltrated Babington's circle, deliberately introducing into his plans the notion of assassinating Elizabeth I. Every coded message sent by Mary to the conspirators was intercepted and read by Walsingham's men. When her reply implicitly consenting to the assassination fell into their hands, they were triumphant. The agent who decoded her letter saw at once that she had fallen into their trap, and drew a gallows on the letter. To make her message doubly incriminating, Walsingham forged a postscript by which Mary apparently asked for details of the men who were to kill Elizabeth. Her fate was sealed. She was taken to Fotheringhay Castle, tried and sentenced to death.

So how did James react when he heard what was happening? During those difficult days, he ordered Patrick Adamson, the Protestant Archbishop of St Andrews, to pray for her at the Sunday service in Edinburgh's parish church of St Giles', which he himself usually attended. Because of a running dispute about whether there should be bishops in the Church of Scotland, the very mention of the archbishop caused trouble, and one of the regular ministers of St Giles' was already defiantly occupying the pulpit when James and the archbishop arrived. Disconcerted, James said that he could stay, provided he prayed for Mary. The minister refused and left, along with many of the congregation.

This incident probably tells us more about contemporary attitudes towards church government than it does about James's personal feelings. Some commentators believe that he was trying to appease Mary's supporters but, of course, there was also the fact that the death of his mother on the orders of a foreign ruler would have been a very public affront to his own position. Whatever his motives, James could hardly risk losing his chance of being named as Elizabeth's successor by protesting too violently against his mother's death sentence. In the end, Mary was executed at Fotheringhay on 8 February 1587. It was six days before James heard the news, and of course everyone watched with interest to see his reaction. Unfortunately, the descriptions which have survived are not enlightening for, while some reports said that he was deeply upset, others alleged that he was quite unperturbed, and there were those who thought that he put on a show of grief while privately rejoicing.

Eye-witness accounts apart, we know that James refused to receive any messages from England. He ordered his courtiers to wear mourning and, when he finally agreed to accept a letter from Elizabeth, which proved to be full of excuses, he demanded that she give him full satisfaction by recognising him as her heir. This she did not do. Although there were rumours of French and Spanish troops being mobilised to help him to invade England and seek revenge, nothing came of them, and it was not until Elizabeth's death in 1603 that James finally succeeded to her throne. In so doing, he achieved the ambition which he and his mother had each nurtured for so long.

King James VI and I was then determined to rehabilitate his mother's reputation. Mary, Queen of Scots had been buried opposite the tomb of Catherine of Aragon in Peterborough Cathedral, the nearest great church to Fotheringhay. When he arrived in England, James sent a velvet pall to be hung over her grave and immediately made plans to have her coffin interred in a more significant place. This did not happen until 1612, when he gave orders for her coffin to be exhumed and transported slowly to London. The empty space beneath which she had once lain can be seen to this day in Peterborough Cathedral, but her body now rests in a vault under the south aisle of Henry VII's chapel in Westminster Abbey. The magnificent monument which James commissioned for her faces the slightly smaller and much less expensive one which he had commissioned to be erected to Elizabeth I. Mary's effigy in white marble, carved by Cornelius Cure, the royal master mason, and completed by his son William, lies beneath an imposing arch which is surmounted by her coat of arms.

James could have left his mother's remains languishing in comparative obscurity at Peterborough, hoping that people would forget the scandals which had ruined her reputation. By placing them so prominently beside her Tudor ancestors, he was obviously emphasising his own right to the English throne. However, the fact that he was willing to acknowledge her so publicly does suggest that, in his mind, she had not been involved in the murder of his father, as her enemies wanted everyone to believe. Indeed, beneath his political motives there may have lurked something rather different and more personal: a sense of kinship with the woman who had not only been a fellow monarch but had given birth to him.

Chapter 10

Conclusion:
Was Mary, Queen of Scots a silly,
spoilt child all her life?

MYTH

Mary, Queen of Scots was a stupid person who had an easy time of it when she was young. She was spoiled by her family and friends and led a sheltered life at the French court. As a result, she had no idea of how to cope with life, let alone rule a country and, when she came back to Scotland, she made one mistake after another. If her life ended in tragedy, she brought it on herself.

FACTS

A famous painting of Mary, Queen of Scots hangs in Blairs Museum, five miles outside Aberdeen. It is an impressive, full-length portrait showing her in a long black dress and a white cap and ruff, standing on the scaffold before her execution, a crucifix in her right hand and a prayer book in her left. There are two small scenes in the background. One shows the moment when she was beheaded, while the other depicts two of her sorrowing ladies weeping as they watched. The picture was not, of course, done from life, but was commissioned some years afterwards by one of the two ladies, Elizabeth Curle, by that time living in exile in Antwerp.

The queen's features were probably copied from a miniature in Elizabeth Curle's possession. To make clear the message of the painting, several inscriptions in Latin describe how Mary had sought sanctuary in England, only to be held prisoner and executed. They go on to say that, because she was the daughter, wife and mother of kings, no one had any jurisdiction over her, and so her trial and execution were unjust, and they emphasise that she was always a faithful daughter of the Roman Catholic Church. This handsome painting could be described as a propaganda piece for, if Mary had provoked controversy during her lifetime, it redoubled after her death, and for more than 400 years she has been the subject of constant debate. Was she an evil woman and an incompetent ruler, or was she an accomplished monarch who was betrayed by the people who should have been her friends?

At first, the arguments surrounding Mary's life were centred on religion. Catholic writers viewed her as a martyr for her faith, whereas Protestants lost no time in condemning her as a wicked enemy of the Reformed Church who led a totally immoral life. In our own time, the focus has shifted to her personality. Some historians declare that, when she was a child, she was petted and indulged by everyone around her, with the result that she was totally incapable of ruling any country. One recent biographer has even complained that Mary behaved very badly at her coronation, screaming constantly. He did not say that she was just nine months old. Other writers have gone to the opposite extreme, portraying her instead as someone who could do no wrong but was at the mercy of impossible circumstances. The reality shows a more complex and a more formidable personality.

When Mary arrived in England in the spring of 1568, fleeing after the Battle of Langside, Queen Elizabeth sent her envoy Sir Francis Knollys, a profoundly convinced Protestant, to see her. He was obviously expecting to meet a desperate, tattered fugitive, but instead he was impressed in spite of himself. The woman he met was self-confident, talkative and very conscious of her royal position. This lady and princess was, he said respectfully, a notable woman. Desperate for revenge on her enemies, she seemed eager to endure all manner of danger in pursuit of victory over them. Towering above most of the people around her, she presented a majestic figure even though she had cut off her long auburn hair in order to disguise herself during her flight. At 25 years of age, she was strong and vigorous. Nor was this the first time she had shown initiative and decisiveness at a time of crisis, qualities perhaps all the more surprising in one who had inherited her father's highly-strung nature along with her mother's courage and determination.

Mary, it is true, had been a much-loved and admired child but, as we have seen, her early years had not been without their troubles. After all, her father had died when she was only six days old, and her first years were overshadowed by the danger of an invasion of Scotland by the English. Certainly, she was sent to the safety of France when she was five, but that meant a traumatic parting from her much-loved mother, Mary of Guise. Even though she was welcomed and admired at the French court, her life there was not without complications, with the obligation to have her position as a queen in her own right constantly asserted and the need to tread with care amid the petty jealousies of her own and the French royal households. Looking back on those years, it may seem to us that she had nothing to worry about because her future as the next queen consort of France was secure, but it did not appear to be so at the time.

Stupid, Mary was not. Anyone who has read her letters can see at once that they were written by an intelligent person with an unusually high level of verbal fluency. She is often criticised for lacking the political calculation of Elizabeth I, but they were very different personalities, and there is more than one kind of intelligence. During her French childhood, Mary had received the education of a Renaissance princess, studying Latin, Greek, Italian and Spanish as well as drawing, dancing and playing on musical instruments. She learned the neat, italic handwriting fashionable in court circles and, if her strong feelings transformed the even, precise script of her youth into a large and often untidy scrawl in later years, she expressed herself with a passionate eloquence which her English captors would come to dread.

Her interest in language was not merely something forced upon her in the schoolroom. When she came to Scotland, she brought with her books in French, Latin, Italian, Spanish and Greek and kept them in a special library furnished with a green carpet at Holyroodhouse. She possessed about 300 books in all, an enormous amount for that time, particularly for a woman, since most sixteenth-century women were illiterate. Each day after dinner, she read Latin with George Buchanan the classical scholar, and, when she made her will, she planned to leave half of her Greek and Latin books to St Andrews University. As well as the classics, her collection included history and those books on religious controversy which we noted in Chapter 3. For lighter moments, there was her favourite poetry and various romances, stirring tales of past military deeds. All these volumes were left behind when she fled to England in 1568, but reading was her great consolation during her captivity. She gave orders for volumes to her friends and servants, and rebuilt her collection to the extent that those responsible for her complained bitterly about the cartloads of books which she insisted on taking with her whenever she was moved from one place to the next.

The dramas of Mary's personal life have often distracted attention from her performance as ruler of her kingdom. As Michael Lynch has pointed out, she did not neglect the business of governing Scotland during her personal rule. She has been criticised for failing to attend meetings of her Privy Council on a regular basis, but there was nothing unusual about that. Queen Elizabeth I was not a regular attender at her Privy Council's meetings either. Mary covered a far larger area of her country during her progresses, which were not some sort of summer holiday but were intended to bring justice to the areas she visited, and she continued her mother's policy of trying to enforce royal authority throughout Scotland. After the long years of impoverishment during Mary of Guise's regency, where the money for royal conspicuous consumption had been directed into expenditure on soldiers and weapons, her daughter re-established the court as a centre of pageantry and sophisticated entertainment in order to emphasise the power of the monarchy. She worked hard, if in vain, to reconcile her constantly quarrelling nobles, and she determinedly although unsuccessfully tried to persuade them to return to the Roman Catholic faith.

Mary was well trained in social skills. In a small incident after the death of her father-in-law Henri II in 1559, we already have a glimpse of her dignified and authoritative manner. Usually inscrutable and reserved, her mother-in-law Catherine de Medici was devastated by the death of the husband she had loved so much and who had given her so much pain by his affairs with other women. When a procession of visitors came to offer their condolences to the widowed queen, she was so overcome that she could not answer them and it was 16-year-old Mary, sitting at her side, who calmly took charge and conducted the various interviews.

Mary's cool resourcefulness in more violent times of crisis has also been generally played down. It was very evident in, for example, the dangerous hours after the murder of David Rizzio. Despite her shock and the fact that she was well advanced in pregnancy, Mary had not given way. She wept bitterly, it is true, but she saw what needed to be done. She was furious with Darnley for his part in the crime, but she somehow managed to win him over to her side again. Perhaps it was not so difficult to do, for she was by far the stronger character. Desperate to escape from the assassins, who were holding the two of them prisoner in the Palace of Holyroodhouse, Mary sensibly rejected Bothwell's and

Huntly's suggestion that she escape through a window and be lowered to the ground by means of ropes tied to a chair. Instead, she spoke to her captors with great self-possession during the next two days, promising to pardon them and distracting them from her own plan to escape. Pretending to have labour pains, she summoned the midwife the lords had selected for her, persuaded the woman to say that she was dangerously ill, and at midnight crept down the stairs and out of the palace, with Darnley at her heels, leading him to a nearby spot where men were waiting for them with horses.

There then followed a nightmare ride to Dunbar Castle. Because of her condition, Mary rode pillion behind Arthur Erskine, the Captain of the Guard who had been present in the supper chamber when Rizzio was murdered. Darnley, beside himself with fear, kept turning back and whipping their horse, shouting at them to go faster or else he and the queen would both be murdered. When Mary protested and said he was putting their unborn baby in danger, he told her brutally that, if the child died, they could easily have more. In the end she told him to ride on and look after himself, which he did. It took them five hours to cover the twenty-five miles to Dunbar as the crow flies. She described in a letter to Queen Elizabeth afterwards how she had felt dreadful and frequently had to dismount and be sick on the way. However, they arrived at last. Mary had saved the lives of herself, Darnley and their child, her supporters began to flock to her and, nine days after Rizzio's murder, she was able to enter Edinburgh once more.

Another example of her perseverance came when she was imprisoned on the island of Lochleven. She was determined to escape and, at some unknown date in the spring of 1568, she disguised herself as one of the laundresses who came to the castle and made off in the boat which would have taken the woman back to the shore. Her plan was ruined when the boatman noticed her soft white hands, not those of any washerwoman, and she was returned to the castle. The boatman, however, did not tell anyone what had happened and, a few weeks later, there was another attempt, successful this time. A careful plan was made with the help of Willie Douglas, a young relative of the castle's owner, Sir William Douglas. Disguised in a long red gown which belonged to one of her women, with a cloak over it and a hood, the queen walked from the castle, climbed into a boat and hid beneath the boatman's seat. This time, no one stopped her, and she reached the shore, where her friends were waiting with horses. She then rode off to join her supporters.

Mary, Queen of Scots certainly did not lack physical courage. She was sensitive and squeamish, hating bloodshed, and she had collapsed in hysterical tears at the brutal execution of Sir John Gordon, the Earl of Huntly's youthful son, but she was perfectly prepared to ride at the head of her army when occasion demanded. Elizabeth I has been much praised for her rousing speech to her troops at Tilbury in 1588 during the threat of invasion by the Spanish Armada, but Mary was far closer to military action than that. The first time was when, on her summer progress to the north-east of Scotland in 1562, she turned on Huntly, her most powerful Catholic subject. He had already annoyed her by refusing to support her plans for a meeting with Elizabeth I, and now he not only welcomed her to his part of the country with an escort of 1,500 men when he was supposed to bring no more than 100, but he even went on to refuse to open the gates of his castles to her. Mary had no hesitation in moving against him at the head of her army and Thomas Randolph the English ambassador, who had been accompanying her on the progress, told Sir William Cecil that he had never seen her merrier, completely undismayed. He was surprised, he said, for he had not thought she would have the stomach for that sort of action. She is even said to have remarked that she wished she were a man, so that she could stride along in a leather tunic and a helmet.

Next time, she did wear a helmet and had a pistol tucked into her belt as she rode at the head of her forces, her new husband Lord Darnley by her side, in pursuit of her half-brother the Earl of Moray who had rebelled against her. This event came to be known as the 'Chaseabout Raid', for the royal army pursued him first to the west and then back to Edinburgh. The campaign ended when he and his friends managed to slip across the Border into England. This was not exactly a triumph for Mary, and endless trouble would ensue, but at least she was able to congratulate herself on having driven her rebels out of the country. In even more dire circumstances, she was willing to act as she believed a monarch should. A month after her marriage to Bothwell, she took the field against her rebellious Protestant lords at Carberry Hill. Their army was drawn up on the hill opposite, and all day they faced each other as one attempt after another at negotiation failed. As the afternoon passed, Mary's troops began to drift off and she decided to take what she regarded as the honourable way out. It was defeat, of course, but her decision to surrender to the enemy required a good deal of bravery.

The end came when, having escaped from Lochleven, she decided to try to crush her enemies in battle as a king would have done, rather than attempting to enforce her authority by more peaceful means. The two armies confronted each other at Langside, near Glasgow. Watching the conflict from a nearby hillside, Mary could see that her forces were being driven back. She mounted her horse and rode down to urge her soldiers on. One of her retinue later told Catherine de Medici that the queen would have led her men personally in a new charge if she had not found them quarrelling violently among themselves. At that, her courage deserted her for the first time, and she agreed to flee with a small group of supporters led by Lord Herries.

A month later, she described their flight to England in a letter to her uncle, the Cardinal of Lorraine. They rode for ninety-two miles without stopping, she wrote, and then they slept on the ground with only sour milk and oatmeal for sustenance for the next three nights. There was not one other woman with them, something shocking to Mary, who had spent all her life with her ladies-in-waiting around her. When they reached Lord Herries's stronghold of Terregles, they held a council of war, and her companions were appalled when she insisted on going to England to see Elizabeth I in person. No English monarch could be trusted, they said, and they begged her to sail to France instead. By her own account, she would not listen, vowing to be back in Scotland again in three months' time at the head of an army which she was confident would be supplied by Elizabeth I. Next day, they crossed the Solway into England.

It was hardly surprising that Mary was involved in plans for her escape during the long years of her English captivity, but, throughout the turmoil of her life, she retained a strong sense of her own majesty. It was not that she was a silly young girl who said: 'Don't speak to me like that. I am a queen.' It was a far deeper and more meaningful aspect of her nature. She believed that, from infancy, she had been set apart as a monarch, chosen by God to rule her native land and that conviction gave her a dignity and a compulsion to show leadership in whatever situation she found herself. Descriptions of her uncharacteristically meek and submissive behaviour towards Bothwell may have been true, but they are unreliable, coming as they do in part from the envious courtiers who were his enemies and in part from later commentators who were desperate to make excuses for her fatal decision to marry him, arguing that her allegedly strange and altered manner was a sign of nervous collapse.

In Western Europe's patriarchal society, most men firmly believed that no female had the right to rule, and her lords were all too ready to take advantage of Mary's youth and inexperience to further their own ambitions. Her mature and effective mother had in the end lost her long struggle to impose her authority on the Scots, and an attractive and headstrong young woman recently returned from a foreign country was all the more vulnerable. However, Mary, Queen of Scots was far from being some poor, downtrodden victim. She was a larger-than-life personality in every way, not only physically but also in the strength of her emotions, in the vigour with which she expressed her thoughts and in her concept of her own role. Even throughout her English years as a frustrated prisoner in declining health, she was insistent on maintaining the symbols of her royalty, such as her cloth of state. Although she dressed in black, with rosaries, crucifixes or brooches with a religious theme as her only jewellery, she was still an imposing figure. She remained to the end a queen in her own mind, and, when she mounted the scaffold at the age of 44 and placed her neck on the block, she did so with dignity and without a hint of fear.

Further reading

John Guy, 'My Heart is my Own': The Life of Mary, Queen of Scots (London, 2004) is a detailed, sympathetic biography of Mary, Queen of Scots; and Antonia Fraser, Mary, Queen of Scots (London, 1969) remains a classic account. Leading the charge against Mary is Jenny Wormald, Mary, Queen of Scots: A Study in Failure (London, 1991). Different aspects of the reign are covered by Marcus Merriman, The Rough Wooings: Mary, Queen of Scots 1542–1551 (East Linton, 2000); Rosalind K. Marshall, Queen Mary's Women: Female Relatives, Servants, Friends and Enemies of Mary, Queen of Scots (Edinburgh, 2006); Gordon Donaldson, The First Trial of Mary, Queen of Scots (London, 1969); A. E. MacRobert, Mary, Queen of Scots and the Casket Letters (London, 2002); Mary Stewart, Queen in Three Kingdoms, ed. Michael Lynch (Oxford, 1988); and Julian Sharman, The Library of Mary, Queen of Scots (London, 1889). For the text of Friedrich Schiller's play, there is Peter Oswald, Schiller's Mary Stuart in a New Version (London, 2006).

More can be read about Mary's husbands and contemporaries in Caroline Bingham, Darnley: A Life of Henry Stuart, Lord Darnley, Consort of Mary Queen of Scots (London, 1995); Robert Gore-Browne, Lord Bothwell (London, 1937);

Rosalind K. Marshall, *Mary of Guise, Queen of Scots* (Edinburgh, 2001); Alan Stewart, *The Cradle King: A Life of James VI and I* (London, 2003); Maurice Lee Jr, *James Stewart, Earl of Moray* (New York, 1953); Rosalind K. Marshall, *John Knox* (Edinburgh, 2000); and David Tweedie, *David Rizzio and Mary, Queen of Scots: Murder at Holyrood* (Stroud, 2006). The *Oxford Dictionary of National Biography* (Oxford, 2004) includes entries for these people and many others mentioned in this text.

Index